Amir Muzur, Iva Rinčić

Van Rensselaer Potter and His Place in the History of Bioethics

Ethik in der Praxis/Practical Ethics

Studien/Studies

herausgegeben von

Ilhan Ilkilic
Universität Istanbul

Arnd T. May
Erfurt

Amir Muzur
Universität Rijeka

Hans-Martin Sass
Ruhr-Universität Bochum,
Georgetown University Washington DC

Martin Woesler
Universität Witten/Herdecke

Band 42

LIT

Amir Muzur, Iva Rinčić

Van Rensselaer Potter and His Place in the History of Bioethics

LIT

Cover image: Erwin J. Löhr

This book is an updated and abridged English version of the Croatian edition that was published in December 2015 by the Pergamena publishing company of Zagreb.

English translation by: Adverbum, d. o. o. Opatija

Bibliographic information published by the Deutsche Nationalbibliothek
The Deutsche Nationalbibliothek lists this publication in the Deutsche Nationalbibliografie; detailed bibliographic data are available on the Internet at http://dnb.d-nb.de.

ISBN 978-3-643-91133-9 (pb)
ISBN 978-3-643-96133-4 (PDF)

A catalogue record for this book is available from the British Library.

Klosbachstr. 107
CH-8032 Zürich
Tel. +41 (0) 44-251 75 05
E-Mail: zuerich@lit-verlag.ch http://www.lit-verlag.ch
Distribution:
In the UK: Global Book Marketing, e-mail: mo@centralbooks.com
In North America: Independent Publishers Group, e-mail: orders@ipgbook.com
In Germany: LIT Verlag Fresnostr. 2, D-48159 Münster
Tel. +49 (0) 2 51-620 32 22, Fax +49 (0) 2 51-922 60 99, e-mail: vertrieb@lit-verlag.de
e-books are available at www.litwebshop.de

TABLE OF CONTENTS

ACKNOWLEDGEMENTS

It is said that a common trait of all the dissertations at Madison McArdle is to put Bette Sheehan, the long-time department secretary, in first place in the acknowledgements section. Our first encounter with Bette, whom we previously knew only via electronic correspondence, happened at the small Madison airport in the late hours of a late September day in 2014. Bette waited for us patiently despite our flight being delayed, fought bravely for our lost luggage, and finally accompanied us to our boarding house on Lake Mendot with a bag full of local cheeses and beers. Little did we know that this warm but rarely smiling 'good soul' of McArdle would make our five days in Madison much more mobile and efficient, thanks to her knowledge of the place, people, and history, which went well beyond usual courtesy and hospitality. Well, dear Bette, let the first acknowledgement, according to custom, be for you.

Both in and around Madison, other people who did not know us – Jim Shull, Paul Lambert, Henry Pitot, Roz Boutwell, Dick Burgess, Olga Trubetskoy, Dave Nelson, Sue Lederer, Michael Schuler and Joyce Probstein – kindly accepted us and devoted their time to us. Kathy and Toby Potter welcomed us at their estate in Portage, and Cal and Ruth DeWitt in Dunn. Although we missed the opportunity to meet him in Madison, Aldo Leopold's biographer Curt Meine sent us his articles, which were still unpublished at the time.

Lisa Potter and Margaret Doris (who sent us her, then freshly defended, dissertation) gave us plenty of advice, even though we did not meet them in person.

In Washington, we were welcomed just as warmheartedly: Laura Bishop opened to us all the doors of the Kennedy Institute of Ethics, Martina Darragh with her associates made all the shelves of the Institute's real and virtual libraries available to us, and Warren Reich shared with us many of his memories.

Our trip to the United States would not of course have been possible without the project support of the University of Rijeka and the City of Rijeka, for which we personally thank the mayor, Vojko Obersnel.

Regarding this book, the list of people to whom we are grateful is long and well-established: from the reviewers and the publisher Ante Selak and his associates, who worked with accuracy and enthusiasm, to our tireless and restless editor Ante Čović, with whom ideas were discussed on the phone into the late evening hours (as a result of which, the conclusion of one discussion usually opened up another one).

All the aforementioned ladies and gentlemen have made working on this book so easy that it has been hard to believe, and so pleasant that we feel a little bit guilty.

FOREWORD

After thorough research into the life and work of Fritz Jahr (which resulted in three books and a number of articles, conferences in Rijeka, São Paulo and Halle, the translation of Jahr's entire opus into Croatian, and a more or less rounded biography and bibliography, but sadly without finding his portrait), it seemed logical to tackle another subject that was close to this one so that we could make use of our previous work, but which was also fresh enough to avoid falling into the trap of futilely moving in circles without adding any new material. (Apart from new pieces of information, new material may also include new hypotheses, even if such new hypotheses are too rare to be taken as the main basis of a book). And so we decided to tackle the life and work of Van Rensselaer Potter, another father of bioethics. Surprisingly (to some extent, of course, also fortunately for us), Potter proved to be almost as unresearched as Jahr had been ten years before. On the internet, one could only find a few lines concerning his life and a short biography on the pages of the McArdle, his home institution for cancer research at the University of Wisconsin in Madison. A few articles dealt with Potter's work (Ivan Šegota,[1] Peter Whitehouse,[2] Hrvoje Jurić,[3] Henk ten Have[4] and others) but barely mentioned his life, while the other few were reminiscences deprived of objectivity and research. Therefore, the first real discovery for us was the dissertation of Boston theologian Margaret Doris, defended in April 2014 after years of research, which finally provided a more detailed biography of Potter (admittedly in the context of a somewhat forced and therefore very simplified attempt to connect his bioethics with certain elements of American tradition). Apart from the fact that it did not include any photographic documentation, it also turned out that Doris had not taken a look into the 'Ali Baba's Cave' of Potter's personal archive, which is kept in twenty boxes at the McArdle. We were lucky enough to explore this 'cave' at the best possible time: while its contents were being packed in order to be delivered to the University archives and while it was being managed

---

[1] Cf. Ivan Šegota, 'Intervjui: Van Rensselaer Potter, Rihito Kimura, Albert Jonsen, Hyakudai Sakamoto' ['Interviews: Van Rensselaer Potter, Rihito Kimura, Albert Jonsen, Hyakudai Sakamoto'], *Bioetički svesci* 19 (1999).

[2] Cf. Peter J. Whitehouse, 'The rebirth of bioethics: Extending the original formulations of Van Rensselaer Potter', *American Journal of Bioethics* 3, no. 4 (2003): W26-W31.

[3] Cf. Hrvoje Jurić, 'Uporišta za integrativnu bioetiku u djelu Van Rensselaera Pottera' ['The basis for integrative bioethics in the work of Van Rensselaer Potter'], in *Integrativna bioetika i izazovi suvremene civilizacije: zbornik radova Prvog međunarodnog bioetičkog simpozija u Bosni i Hercegovini (Sarajevo, 31. III.–1. IV. 2006.)* [*Integrative Bioethics and the Challenges of Modern Civilisation: Proceedings of the First International Bioethics Symposium in Bosnia and Herzegovina (Sarajevo 31.03.-01.04.2006)*], ed. Velimir Valjan (Sarajevo: Bioetičko društvo u BiH, 2007), 77-99.

[4] Henk A. M. J. ten Have, 'Potter's notion of bioethics', *Kennedy Institute of Ethics Journal* 22, no. 1 (2012): 59-82.

by Bette Sheehan, who made it available to us together with Potter's manuscripts, correspondence, library and photo albums. Sue Lederer, Head of the Department of History of Medicine and Bioethics of the University of Wisconsin Madison Medical School, whose office is located in a building right next to the McArdle, had just recently found out about Potter's archives and had not had time to explore them yet, even though she – in a conversation with us – basically expressed her desire and plans to do so.

And so we have, completely by accident, just as in Halle, managed to make use of a source available to many who actually were here every day before us. During countless discussions, archive searches, readings, and mutual provocations, we changed our impressions of Potter several times. Sometimes he seemed brilliant to us, and sometimes we thought that he was just skilfully modifying other people's ideas. For a moment, we admired him without criticism, and a second later we pitied and even judged him. Still, our research showed (as it had many times before) that there is no material more fascinating than the biographic: the details about someone's life journey – communication with his contemporaries; family, educational and professional circumstances; beliefs and dreams; maturation and transformation – all lead us to a state which goes beyond mere interest in the subject and transcends itself to some extent into an identification with the researched person. Of course, while it brings fuel and passion for further research, it can also bring bias. However, didn't John Eccles claim that science is the most subjective human activity known to him? If researching someone's life and work counts as science, then it is exactly like that: a self-permeating, all-permeating passion. We can only believe that it is useful to others as well: that someone's life really explains his or her work, that it helps us to understand and also use it correctly. Those who don't believe in the benefits of biographies should just remember how many things they have done based on their mood, family worries, jealousies and envies, and likes and dislikes; how much energy they have found in themselves on 'good days' and how much has been lost on 'bad' ones; how many people they have neglected because they wanted to avoid them (at least in what they were doing), and how many they have overemphasised by rewarding them; how many activities they have interrupted because they couldn't do anything different at a given moment, and how many jobs they have accepted because they were offered by someone whom they could not refuse. The biography of a thinker is the key to reading most of their thoughts. In this book, we shall try, among other things, to prove this to all the hypothetical doubting Thomases out there.

FROM BIO-CHEMISTRY TO BIO-ETHICS: THE LIFE AND WORK OF VAN RENSSELAER POTTER[1]

Although he was not the first in history to use the term 'bioethics', Van Rensselaer Potter II is definitely one of the most important people in the history of this discipline. It is therefore somewhat unbelievable how little data is available on his life. No book or comprehensive biographical article has been published about him; the all-knowing, all-revealing and all-covering English *Wikipedia* includes only five lines under his name, and the Spanish version nine lines. What is the reason for this ignorance and neglect of the person who in North America (at least when it is suitable) is still celebrated as the founder of bioethics, and who by some was even seriously considered as a candidate for the Nobel Prize?

It is not clear where the claim that Van Rensselaer Potter was of Dutch descent came from.[2] The European blood which is, at least for the moment, easier to prove, is Irish. The oldest Potter that we know about was our Van's great grandfather, David H. (born in 1822), who on 23 November 1848 married Malinda/Melinda Lindsay/Lindsey (born in 1829). David and Malinda first lived in their hometown of Tuscarawas in Coshocton County, Ohio, and they had four children: Andrew H. (born in 1850), S. J. (born in 1851), C. S. (born in 1853), and Van Rensselaer (1859-1910, grandfather of 'our' Potter, who was named after him and received the attribute the 'Second').[3] Van Rensselaer Potter I was born in the town to which his parents had moved in 1851: Wethersfield in Henry

---

[1] An earlier and significantly shorter version of the first part of this chapter was presented at the 13th Lošinj Days of Bioethics (Mali Lošinj, 18-21 May 2014), entitled 'Van Rensselaer Potter (1911-2001): Contribution toward research of life and intellectual evolution of the 'stepfather' of bioethics'.

[2] It is possible that this came from the bioethicist Henk ten Have, a Dutchman himself. 'Van Rensselaer' is the name of a family of Dutch feudal lords (*patroons*) who in the first half of the 17th century had large land holdings in the northeast of what is today the USA (formerly New Holland). This family, which provided the American Revolution with several military leaders, also gave its name to the town of Rensselaer (c. 10,000 inhabitants), which is separated from Albany, the capital of the state of New York, by the River Hudson. Today, the small town of Rensselaer is the seat of an old institute for technology and the pharmaceutical and chemical industries.

In America, when two families joined and one side was without a male heir, it was not unusual for that side to retain their surname (e.g. Van Rensselaer) as a personal name. Although V. R. Potter II believed that this is what had happened, it seems unlikely that the Potters, who were among the first English settlers in America, and who would later side with the Revolution, would be associated with the counterrevolutionary Dutch Van Rensselaers.

[3] Six brothers and sisters are mentioned somewhere (Happy, Ingabee, King David and others). Cf. *Pierpoint Centennial: 1887-1987* (Pierpont: Langford Bugle, 1987), 311.

County, Illinois. Van Rensselaer continued to move west at the age of twenty three, when he established his home in the village of Andover in Day County in South Dakota after marrying (on Christmas Eve 1882) Jennie Tobin (1859-1943), the daughter of Irish immigrants to Macomb in Illinois.

Jennie and Van Rensselaer (I) lived on a farm and had two sons: Floyd V. (October 1883-1946) and Arthur Howard (Broadacres near Pierpont, 27 March 1888 – August 1962), the future father of V. R. Potter II. It seems that the family did rather well, since in 1900 they had a maid (sixteen-year-old Julia Olesen from Minnesota), and by 1910 a maid (nineteen-year-old Emilia Knudson) and three servants (Charley Tobin – probably a cousin of Jennie, Charley Spilman, and Harry Thomas, who were between 20 and 42 years old). Moreover, in 1907 the couple celebrated the silver anniversary of their estate with printed invitations and a hired orchestra. Their son Floyd also worked on the farm, just like his father, while Arthur first acquired an education (he learned steam engineering at the State College in Brookings but dreamt about architecture), and then, at the age of 29, reluctantly and at his parents' urging, continued as a farmer (like his brother Floyd).[4] Apparently, he did this in a very innovative way, but still this constraint must have resulted in Arthur's determination to ensure a different kind of life for his son. Tall, slim, and dark-haired, Arthur was exempted from mobilisation in 1917 because of a broken arcade. After a period of seven years of drought and plagues of locusts, the Potter farm, which in around 1909 had encompassed an area of more than 800 acres, was ruined and eventually abandoned by 1934.

Arthur Howard 'Herbert' was first married on 24 November 1908 to Julia Eva 'Bobby' Herpel (daughter of John C. and Julia, natives of Michigan). She bore a son, Van Rensselaer II (who inherited this name from his grandfather, who had died of stomach cancer a year earlier), in August 1911. After Eva died in a car accident in November 1917 (as she was driving with her husband from Pierpont, where they had gone to see a movie), Arthur married for a second time on 2 December 1919, this time to the pharmacist Anna Sivertson (1894-1960), who worked in her father's pharmacy in Pierpont, and with whom he had two daughters (V. R. Potter's half-sisters), Jean Delight (born in 1924) and Ruth Ann (born in 1927). His stepmother tried to steer the young Van in the direction of chemistry and even organised a 'course' on advanced pharmacology in the office of the dean of the Faculty of Pharmacy, who was her school colleague (Anna

[4] Floyd would marry the sister of Arthur's wife, Daisy Herpel, 'the first white child' born in Andover (to where her parents had moved to in 1882 in search of a better climate for her father's tuberculosis). Both parents of Daisy Herpel, i.e. the grandmother and grandfather of V. R. Potter on his mother' side, died of cancer in 1936 and 1941. Cf. Margaret E. Doris, 'Land-Grant Ideology, the Wisconsin Idea, and the Foundations of Van Rensselaer Potter's Bioethics' (PhD thesis, Boston University Faculty of Theology, 2014), 115-116. Floyd's children were Arthur John (born in 1911 like V. Rensselaer), Richard Louis and Helen.

Sivertson had graduated in 1914 as the only woman in her year). Arthur Howard moved to where Anna was in Pierpont, and they built a house on the main street whose seven rooms on the second floor they turned into the *Biltmore* guesthouse (after the New York hotel of the same name). At the same time, in 1920, they had in their household in Andover a hired worker William Bull (36 years old) from Kansas. After a failed attempt to run a store and the occurrence of a fire in the café on the first floor of the house in Pierpont, they moved in 1934 to Tacoma in the state of Washington. Apart from his wife and their two daughters, Arthur also took his mother (Potter's grandmother Jennie) with him. In Tacoma, Arthur worked in a match factory, and later in the shipyard. At that time, in June 1942, Van Rensselaer wrote to a glass factory in New York asking about possible flash protection for welding, which was his father's job.[5] Arthur Potter moved to a better world at the age of 74. Officially, he had had a warm relationship with his son Van Rensselaer until the end of his life. However, according to Van's son Toby, the relationship between Van and his father Arthur was 'never the same again' after his marriage to Anna Sivertson. Potter's half-sister Jean married John M. Kehl and had daughters, Grace and Katherine, while Ruth Ann married Robert G. Smith, with whom she had Steven Howard.

Van Rensselaer Potter II was raised in the Presbyterian faith, spent time with his mother's sister, that is, his aunt Daisy, and her children (that is, his 'double' cousins), and financed his education thanks to his father's ambition,[6] help or loans from his two grandmothers (to the amount of 800 dollars), and by selling popcorn at the local theatre (his savings of 450 dollars, however, were lost after the bank went bankrupt). In 1928, he graduated from high school in Pierpont,[7] and in 1933 obtained the title of *Bachelor of Science (BSc)* at the South Dakota State College in Brookings (*General Science*), where he began earning some money by washing rat cages at the Experimental Station of the Institute for Chemistry, which was headed by Kurt W. Franke (1889-1936).[8] He later took part in the performance of experiments and the publication of the results. As a student, Potter was also involved in the debate team, writing news, and editing college newspapers, until Franke called him into his office and, after objecting that he was 'doing too many things', made him decide whether he was going to

[5] McArdle Laboratory Archive, V. R. Potter, box no. 11.

[6] According to Potter, his father would stop people on the street and tell them: 'This is my son – the best in the class'. Van Rensselaer Potter II, 'Short autobiographical sketch requested by National Academy of Science 3/13/89, (completed April 2, 1990)', 1-11. McArdle Laboratory Archive, V. R. Potter.

[7] It seems that this school left a lasting impression on Potter, as he would happily visit it whenever he returned to the town of his birth.

[8] The type of cages that Franke designed would later be introduced to the institute at Madison by Potter. K. W. Franke died of brucellosis.

be a newspaperman or a chemist.[9] Another 'slap on the wrist' for Potter was when, after criticising the lack of talent of the Dean of Agriculture, he was called by the rector and advised to 'keep his political views on ice until he was a professor'.[10] (It is interesting that Potter later similarly suggested his young associate James Shull should not enter politics until he was a 'name' that others would listen to.)

As we know, Potter developed an interest in chemistry and biology at an early age and stood out for his study of metabolism of selenium and his publications in scientific journals[11] (he won the *ACS Prize Essay Contest* in 1927 as a high school student).[12] Potter's interest in selenium was sparked by Franke, who discovered that this is the only mineral absorbed by plants from the soil to a degree sufficient to become pathogenic and even lethal for grazing animals (so-called alkali disease). Potter enthusiastically presented the results of his initial research on selenium-poisoned rat blood in the early 1930s at the Mayo Clinic in Rochester in Minnesota, where he spent two weeks.

After receiving his bachelor's degree, Potter sent more than 50 applications across the USA to further his studies but to no avail.[13] In the summer of 1934, he went with his friends to Chicago to see the 'Century of Progress' exhibition, which popularised the achievements of (American) science. On the way back, he stopped in Madison. After failing to meet the famous Harry Steenbock, with

[9] Things would change a few years later and Potter became secretary of the student Pi Kappa Delta organisation, and also one of five student representatives on the college supervisory board. The motto of Potter's generation, with its strong faith in the revival of science and economics under the influence of chemistry, was 'A quitter never wins and a winner never quits'. Cf. Doris, 'Land-Grant Ideology', 126.

[10] Cf. Doris, 'Land-Grant Ideology', 120-121.

[11] Cf. Kurt W. Franke and Van R. Potter, 'A new toxicant occurring naturally in certain samples of plant foodstuffs', *The Journal of Nutrition* 8, no. 6 (1934): 615-624; Kurt W. Franke and Van R. Potter, 'The effect of selenium containing foodstuffs on growth and reproduction of rats at various ages', *The Journal of Nutrition* 12, no. 2 (1936): 615-624. However, two older Franke publications (his first) on the toxicity of selenium (also in *The Journal of Nutrition*), do not mention Potter as co-author, although according to Potter he had made a significant contribution. An article on the ability of rats to distinguish between poison and food was published in 1936 in the prestigious magazine *Science* and attracted the attention of the general public. Cf. Kurt W. Franke and Van Rensselaer Potter, 'The ability of rats to discriminate between diets of varying degrees of toxicity', *Science* 83, no. 2153 (1936): 330-332.

[12] The prize included a gold coin of 20 dollars (two and a half dollars bought five volumes of a good chemistry textbook; Potter would keep one of them until the end of his life). The competition was launched in 1923. Francis Garvan was concerned by what he saw as the US lagging behind the patents of the German chemical industry after the war. The prize was dedicated to the memory of his five-year-old daughter Patricia who had died of rheumatic fever.

[13] Potter II, 'Short autobiographical sketch', 6.

whom he had wanted to establish contact, Potter accidentally came across Conrad Elvehjem, who aroused his interest in enzymology, which at the time was very popular in biochemistry (back then it was still called 'biological chemistry').[14] In 1935, a Wisconsin Alumni Research Foundation (WARF)[15] scholarship for scientific research enabled Potter to enter the University of Wisconsin Department for Biochemistry, which was headed by Elvehjem. Conrad Arnold 'Connie' Elvehjem (1901-1962) was of Norwegian descent and was born on a small farm in Wisconsin. He went to school in Madison and Cambridge,[16] and after returning to Madison discovered that nicotine acid cured the canine version of pellagra (lack of vitamin B3). When Tom Spies, Marion Blankenhorn and Clark Cooper established that niacin also cured pellagra in humans, and when for their discovery they were named *Time* magazine's 'Men of the Year 1938', Potter fired off a letter to the editor, complaining that they had overlooked Elvehjem's contribution.[17] Later Dean of the Faculty of Medicine and Rector of the University, Elvehjem died of a heart attack while seated at the table.[18] Potter remained faithful to the memory of his teacher and later employed Elvehjem's developmentally disabled son.

The year 1935 brought another novelty to Potter's life. On 3 August 1935, he married his 'college sweetheart' Vivian Christensen in the Student Presbyterian Centre. She was born on 22 September 1915 in Brookings, where Potter went to school. The couple started off very modestly, living separately to save money, and then moved to a rented house in 1940. At that time Potter, with his PhD in agricultural chemistry, which he had gained in 1938 (he had obtained his master's degree in 1936), had an annual salary of 2,700 dollars (he also had some part-time earnings). Vivian, the daughter of Nora and the popular conductor of the South Dakota State College Orchestra, Carl 'Christy',[19] had three years of college behind her (she had graduated in *home economics*) and was a housewife, and with Van Rensselaer had three children: Karin Evangeline

---

[14] Elsewhere, Potter said that a conversation he had had with Elvehjem in 1945 in a hotel room that they were sharing as participants at conference on enzymes was the key factor in him turning towards enzymes. Cf. Van Rensselaer Potter, Oral history no. 257 (Wisconsin University). It is not clear how starting to focus on enzymes in 1945 would take Potter to the top of this area of science in just two years or why such a conversation with Elvehjem would take place ten years after they had started working together.

[15] The Foundation was largely financed with revenue from Steenbock's patent for the discovery of vitamin D, and actively sought scholars throughout the American Midwest.

[16] R. H. Burris, C. A. Baumann and V. R. Potter, 'Conrad Arnold Elvehjem, 1901-1962', *Biographical Memoirs of the National Academy of Sciences* 59 (1990): 135-167.

[17] Doris, 'Land-Grant Ideology', 131-132.

[18] Cf. Van Rensselaer Potter, 'Years with Conrad Elvehjem', in *One Hundred Years of Agricultural Chemistry and Biochemistry at Wisconsin: A Steenbock Symposium*, eds. David L. Nelson and Brook Chase Soltvedt (Madison: Science Tech Publishers, 1989).

[19] He came with his family as a thirteen-year-old to the USA from Copenhagen. He later won awards with the orchestra and headed the Department of Music of the State College.

(born on 1 April 1940; later married as Simon), John Howard (born on 18 May 1943; earlier he lived in Ithaca in the state of New York, and now in Lake Geneva in the extreme southeast of Wisconsin) and Carl 'Toby' Tobin (born on 26 December 1946). They had Potter's six grandchildren, Lisa (married to Bonvicini), Mabs, Joshua, Jeremy, Jesse and Eleanora (married to Archie) Simon (the Simons lived in Boulder in Colorado), and three great-grandchildren, Emma, Britta and Alexander. Carl married a colleague from his studies in Madison, Katherine (Kathy) Tenney, and first taught in a high school and later worked as an electrician. In 1970, the couple moved to a farm in Portage (more precisely, to the slopes of Baraboo, not far from the place where Leopold had lived), and had daughters Lisa in 1971 and Mabs in 1972.

Following the advice that he had received a long time before in answer to his letter to the President of the American Chemistry Society – 'As for university, it doesn't matter where you go but from whom you learn' – he continued his education at the Biochemical Institute in Stockholm, headed by Hans von Euler-Chelpin (1873-1964).[20] In Sweden, he mastered special enzyme chemistry techniques. He loved living there, the forestry laws, outdoor sports, and social progress in general. After he returned to Madison, he introduced the custom of afternoon tea with colleagues. (On a later occasion, in April 1944, Potter was invited to hold a lecture for members of the Rotary Club in Brookings on the subject of 'Finland and Sweden or Finland or Sweden' (from the perspective of South Dakota, these are equally faraway subjects). After the outbreak of World War Two, he renounced further specialisation in England (thanks to a Rockefeller scholarship, he should have continued his work with Hans Adolf Krebs[21] in Sheffield[22]) and went to the University of Chicago to work with Thorfin Hogness (1894-1976).[23] Very soon afterwards, in 1940, he received the position of 'Jonathan Bowman Fellow' (1940-1942), though the

[20] A grant from the American National Scientific Research Council for post-graduate students allowed Potter to go to Stockholm. Von Euler-Chelpin, raised and educated in Germany, worked in Sweden from 1899, and in 1929 won the Nobel Prize for his explanation of the role played by enzymes in the alcoholic fermentation of carbohydrates.

[21] Hans Adolf Krebs (1900-1981) was a German doctor who was a pioneer in the study of the metabolism of urea. As a Jew, he was forced to leave Germany in 1933, initially for Cambridge University, then Sheffield, and finally Oxford. He won the 1953 Nobel Prize for his study of cellular respiration and discovery of the citric acid cycle (the Krebs Cycle).

[22] It is interesting how Potter always mentioned (even in his official CV) that he had worked with Krebs (even though it was only for a month). In fact, on the day that the boat arrived in England, he was recalled to the USA as a result of the outbreak of war. Consequently, it is doubtful whether he even had the time to meet Krebs. The Rockefeller Foundation allowed him to use the scholarship in Chicago, which he did.

[23] As a professor of physical chemistry, T. Hogness participated in the Manhattan Project, which was dedicated to developing an atomic bomb and ballistic missiles, but after World War II, together with Einstein, Szilard and others, he formed the Emergency Committee of Atomic Scientists to warn of the dangers of the misuse of atomic energy.

pay was less, at the McArdle Laboratory for Cancer Research (the laboratory was founded that same year)[24] of the University of Wisconsin in Madison, where he later became assistant principal (1958-1972)[25] and where he remained until his retirement (on 1 July 1982, as Hilldale Professor of Oncology after 1980). On this occasion, on 25 June 1982, a dinner was organised for numerous friends and a pamphlet was printed with the title 'A tribute to Van Rensselaer Potter on his retirement from the University of Wisconsin and the initiation of the Van Rensselaer Potter Lectureship'. In addition to biographical data and a description of Potter's contribution to science, the pamphlet also included a list of Potter's doctoral and post-doctoral students. One of them – Arthur B. Pardee, a Harvard professor of pharmacology and a member of the National Academy of Sciences and American Academy of Arts and Sciences – held the first lecture named after Potter, on the subject of 'The yin and yang of cell growth control'.

As is often the case in America, Potter had the opportunity to change his working environment several times. For example, in December 1941, Clare Chrisman Todd (1880-1954), Head of the Department of Chemistry (and former Dean of the College of Sciences and Arts) offered Potter the position of docent at Washington State College in Pullman. He had two laboratories and two doctoral students available to him, and the opportunity to do exclusively research work, but Potter refused because, in his opinion, the salary was too low. At Elvehjem's recommendation, Leonard Amby Maynard (1887-1972) in September 1942 offered Potter the position of docent at the Graduate School of Nutrition of Cornell University in Ithaca in the state of New York (Maynard was the first director of the school), but gave up on Potter because 'in a conversation he gained the impression that Potter was not willing to leave what he was currently doing'.[26] In February 1943, Potter also refused the invitation of Franklin Chambers McLean (1888-1968),[27] Head of the Department of Physiology of the University of Chicago.

In 1945, the *United States Junior Chamber* ('*Jaycees*')[28] listed Potter among 'ten outstanding young Americans'. In 1947, he won the *Paul-Lewis Laboratories*

---

[24] Potter, the second person to be employed at the Laboratory (after Harold Rusch), was invited to the McArdle by the Dean of the Faculty of Medicine, probably at the urging of Elvehjem, with whom Potter had kept in contact (as early as December 1939, Potter held a lecture at Madison that he had been invited to give on new developments in the study of enzymes). Cf. Doris, 'Land-Grant Ideology', 137-138.

[25] It says somewhere 1959-1978.

[26] McArdle Laboratory Archive, V. R. Potter, box no. 11.

[27] F. C. McLean was also the founder, on behalf of the Rockefeller Foundation, of the Peking Union Medical College. He studied medicine in Vienna and Graz, and participated in the Manhattan Project, investigating the effects of radiation on human tissue.

[28] The organisation, founded in 1920, was aimed at young people between the ages of 18 and 40, and was particularly concerned with promoting leadership qualities. As the result of a court decision, in the 1980s it was forced to accept women. Besides Potter, the prominent ten

Award in Enzyme Chemistry[29] of the American Chemical Society,[30] the *Chemical Bulletin* listed him among the 'ten most prominent biochemists', and the University of Wisconsin awarded him the title of Full Professor of Oncology (he was Assistant Professor from 1942-1945, and Associate Professor from 1945-1947; in 1982, after his retirement, he became Professor Emeritus and continued to go to work every day). In 1959, Potter became an honorary doctor of science at South Dakota State University, in February 1961 he received the Bertner Foundation Award,[31] in April 1964 the American Association for Cancer Research awarded him the G. H. A. Clowes Memorial Award[32] for recent research into cancer biochemistry, in April 1981 he received the Bristol-Myers Award[33] for outstanding achievements in cancer research in the field of chemotherapy development, in 1986 the Medal of Honour of the American Cancer Society, and in 1998 an honorary doctorate from Michigan State University. In October 2000, Brunetto Chiarelli encouraged members of Potter's 'Network' to send letters of support for Potter's candidature for the Kyoto Prize, which is awarded by the Inamori Foundation in three fields – Advanced Technology, Basic Sciences, and Arts and Philosophy – and which is considered by some as the Japanese version of the Nobel Prize. However, Hyakudai Sakamoto, who had unsuccessfully proposed Potter one year before, discouraged the 'Network' by explaining the strict procedure. Still, Sakamoto succeeded in formally proposing Potter in 2001 anew but again without success.[34] In March 2001, Chiarelli started an international campaign to try to nominate Potter for the Nobel Prize and announced the support of the European Association of Global Bioethics, the International Institute for Anthropological

---

of 1945 included Gene Root, Head of the Aerodynamics Department of the *Douglas* company; George C. Dade, president of the transport concern *Dade brothers*; James Linen, publisher of *Time*; Frank McCarthy, Assistant Secretary of State for Foreign Affairs; journalists and industrialists. The following year, Joseph Kennedy made sure that this group included his son, the future US president John F. Kennedy. Cf. Doris, 'Land-Grant Ideology', 151.

[29] Today, the award is called the Pfizer Award in Enzyme Chemistry.

[30] Cf. 'New beachhead in war on cancer reached, U. W.'s Dr. Potter reports', *Wisconsin State Journal*, 17 September 1947. Potter spoke about an enzyme deficiency being a possible source of tumour growth.

[31] Ernst William Bertner (1889-1950) was Head of the Texas Medical Centre from its foundation in 1945. He died of cancer but first volunteered to participate in a series of trials of potential drugs to treat tumours.

[32] The award was named after the founder of the American Association for Cancer Research.

[33] This was an award given by a pharmaceutical company, and was named after the people who had founded the firm in 1858. In 1989, the company merged with *Squibb*, which was reflected in its name.

[34] Hyakudai Sakamoto, e-mail to the 'Global Bioethics Network', dated 24 October 2000. Archive of the *Fritz Jahr* Documentation and Research Centre for European Bioethics at the University of Rijeka. Left by Ivan Šegota. V. R. Potter 1 (DICEB *Fritz Jahr* Archive SuRi – IŠ – VRP 1).

Studies, the Turin Academy of Sciences, and others.[35] Ivan Šegota, however, recalled that some (Šegota thought it was W. Reich) opposed this idea because 'it was not Potter who invented bioethics but some German'. It remains unexplained whether the 'some' mentioned by Šegota had Fritz Jahr in mind or not.

The McArdle Laboratory, which played a crucial role in Potter's life, was founded primarily thanks to the generous legacy of Michael W. McArdle (1874-1935), originally from Wisconsin, director of the (future) *Sunbeam* corporation,[36] who died of cancer. Further donations (for example by the daughter of the late Senator Bowman),[37] as well as federal funds, encouraged the then Dean of the Faculty of Medicine of the University of Wisconsin, William S. Middleton,[38] to have a new building constructed in 1938 that would house the first centre for extensive scientific cancer research at an academic institution in the USA. In charge of the project of establishing the Laboratory was Harold Paul Rusch (1908-1988), who was connected to Wisconsin by birth and education.[39] Rusch also led the construction of the second laboratory building in 1964. Potter took an active part in the final stage of designing this second McArdle building. Although his room was initially on a lower floor and had a couch where he would have a nap every day, his attention was caught, maybe because of the spectacular view beyond Lake Mendota, by the highest floor (he actually moved there towards the end of his career, introduced a red telephone, and put the sign *Do not resuscitate* above the entrance to his room), where he had one part turned into a hall for meetings and lectures. The old building, which housed the Laboratory from 1940 to 1964, was not very remarkable and

---

[35] Brunetto Chiarelli, e-mail to the 'Global Bioethics Network', dated 14 March 2001. DICEB *Fritz Jahr* Archive SuRi – IŠ – VRP 1.

[36] The company was founded at the end of the 19th century as the *Chicago Flexible Shaft Company*, and was involved in the production of tools for shearing sheep. Later, it turned its attention to making electrical appliances, and in 1946 changed its name to the *Sunbeam Corporation.*

[37] Today, the laboratory is mainly financed from the interest from donations, leaving the principal untouched.

[38] Middleton later gave his name to the library, the building commission for which was chaired by Potter.

[39] He was Director of the McArdle Laboratory from its foundation until 1972. After that, up to his retirement in 1978, he headed the Wisconsin Clinical Cancer Center. From 1954 to 1955, he presided over the American Association for Cancer Research. It is interesting that in his memoirs, Rusch mentions that Potter admitted to him that he had recommended him as the director of the new centre. Was Potter perhaps thinking of replacing Rusch as the director of the McArdle? Harold P. Rusch, *Something Attempted, Something Done: A Personal History of Cancer Research at the University of Wisconsin, 1934-1979* (Madison: Wisconsin Medical Alumni Association, 1984), 164. In a message that was read out at the dinner in honour of H. Rusch on 15 June 1979, Potter pointed that Rusch had been very thrifty and that Potter's promotions to more senior positions had never been accompanied by increases in pay.

today bears no sign at all, while the newer and more imposing one, which was the seat of the McArdle from 1964 to 2014, has a façade known as *Tetris* (after the video game), which the designers conceived after they received symbols from Rusch for cancer in different cultures and scripts (from hieroglyphs and the horoscope to modern medicine). In the summer of 2014, the largest part of the Laboratory moved to its most recent building (*The Wisconsin Institute for Medical Research Tower 2* at Highland Avenue, 6th and 7th floors). Potter was not in favour of this relocation of the McArdle, which began back in his time: 'The Millers walked down these corridors!', he used to say of the old (actually the 'middle') building. James (Jim) A. Miller (1915-2000) and Elizabeth (Betty) Cavert Miller (1920-1987) were for Potter 'two chains of DNA', a couple of geniuses who, according to Potter, should have received the Nobel Prize for starting the series of discoveries on carcinogens and DNA back in 1947, that is before Crick and Watson. Just like Potter, they both had WARF scholarships and were later members of the National Academy of Sciences.[40]

During World War Two, both the Laboratory and Potter started paying more attention to other problems apart from the biochemical basis of cancerogenesis. They focused on the study of the role of oxidative phosphorylation in the genesis of irreversible shock in the wounded. Unlike Dean Middleton, who joined Eisenhower's staff, H. Rusch and V. R. Potter remained in Madison during the war. According to Rusch,[41] this happened at the recommendation of the dean. Still, the letters that Potter exchanged in April 1943 with Paul E. Barry from the Ministry of War Logistics Service, located in Milwaukee, indicate that Potter avoided meeting Barry (to whom Potter was recommended as a biochemist) and declared himself as *not available*. When Potter was contacted anew in July 1943 and received in advance the forms to join the armed forces, Potter replied to Major Robert N. McCreary that he was 'still not available since he was co-leader of a project directly connected to war efforts, which will not be finished for a year or longer'.[42] Obviously, V. R. Potter avoided the draft, although he must have been frustrated by the case of his 'double cousin' Richard (Dick) Louis Potter (1918-1960) who put his successful scientific career (he described the feedback mechanism) and work on his PhD thesis on hold to join the naval air force, where he earned a medal for bravery.[43]

In the winter of 1952-53, Potter spent four months in Lima, Morococha and Junín in Peru, where he worked on organising the Alberto Hurtado Laboratory

---

[40] Van Rensselaer Potter, 'Years with Elizabeth and James Miller: In appreciation', in *Biological Reactive Intermediates 111*, eds. James J. Kocsis, David J. Jollow, Charlotte M. Witmer, Judd O. Nelsen and Robert Snyder (New York: Plenum Publishing Corporation, 1986), 1-9.
[41] Rusch, *Something Attempted, Something Done*, 62.
[42] McArdle Laboratory Archive, V. R. Potter, box no. 11.
[43] See the discussion on this in: Doris, 'Land-Grant Ideology', 142-143.

for the study of the enzymes and physiology of adaptation (of guinea pigs) to high altitudes (this was a subject of interest to the US Air Force during the Korean War), obtaining guinea pigs from local people (who had 30 or 40 of them in their courtyards but who did not want to sell more than three) and, generally, had a great time without telephones and meetings. In the last month, he was joined by his wife. After returning to the USA, Potter held a speech at the opening of the new Wisconsin University Centre in April 1958 about new developments in research into the chemical processes associated with the development of cancer.[44]

Potter spent his whole life studying the biochemical basis of malign processes, a field in which he had significant success and worked tirelessly on popularising (for instance, in February 1951 he held a lecture entitled 'Cancer: The known and the unknown'[45] at the 'Freshmen Forum'). Even today, Potter's discovery that a combination of drugs, determined according to the part of the cell which the drugs affect individually, often helps in cancer therapy is still regarded as one of the greatest achievements of the McArdle Laboratory (other major successes of the Laboratory include Roswell Boutwell's discovery that vitamin A helps prevent certain types of cancer, and the discovery of 5-fluorouracil, 5-FU, a drug used in treating several types of cancer of the breast, colon, stomach, etc., which was synthesised by Charles Heidelberger (1920-1983), later professor at South California University).[46] In 1936, Potter innovated the process of obtaining cell isolates and acellular homogenate (the *Potter-Elvehjem homogeniser*),[47] and some twenty years later the so-called *DNA kit* – actually, a paper model of the

---

[44] Van Rensselaer Potter, 'New horizons in cancer research', *Wisconsin Cancer Bulletin* 20, no. 3 (1958): 5-10.

[45] Cf. Van Rensselaer Potter, 'Cancer: The known and the unknown', manuscript dated 13 February 1951. McArdle Laboratory Archive, V. R. Potter. Compare: *Wisconsin State Journal*, 13 and 15 February 1951 (http://jjonz.us/RadioLogs/pagesnfiles/logs_files_RH/1950s_RH/50–54/1951/51rh_02Feb/51–0213-(Tue)_%5BWSJ%5D.pdf; http://jjonz.us/RadioLogs/pagesnfiles/logs_files_RH/1950s_RH/50–54/1951/51rh_02Feb/51–02–15-(Thu)_%5BWSJ%5D.pdf).

[46] Cf. Rebecca Ryan, 'Rebranding basic', *Madison Magazine*, October 2014, 70-85.

[47] Van Rensselaer Potter and Conrad A. Elvehjem, 'A modified method for the study of tissue oxidations', *Journal of Biological Chemistry* 114, no. 2 (1936): 495-504; Van Rensselaer Potter, 'The homogenate technique', *Methods in Medical Research* 1 (1948): 317-336. This homogeniser appears to have been very simple. It looked like a tube with a plunger which would blend the tissue (the piece of tissue was placed in the tube and the plunger was moved up and down by hand while an electric motor rotated the cylinder). Although there are also experts who state that it was useful, the greatest praise for the invention comes from Potter himself. Cf. Van Rensselaer Potter, ed., *Methods in Medical Research*, vol. 1 (Chicago: Year Book Publishers, 1948).

deoxyribonucleic acid double helix.[48] Potter's model was used in 1964 to construct a DNA sculpture in the hall dedicated to invertebrate biology of the American Museum of Natural History in New York, and in 1967 for the design of the fountain in the atrium of the new Centre for Biotechnology (until 1996 it was located in the Middleton Library) of the University of Wisconsin in Madison (actually, Potter's idea was realised for 900 dollars from alumni funds by the young architect Tom Hibben, whose smaller copper models Potter had noticed at the Madison Art Fair). Potter (with Heidelberger) proved the asymmetric metabolism of citric acid, and also certain phosphate coenzymes and metabolic precursors. Further proof of V. R. Potter's capacity for innovation was his 1953 patent for hi-fi loudspeakers, which were distinguished by their small dimensions and simplicity, and which could efficiently reproduce the entire sound spectrum, including low frequencies, in high quality.

In February 1945, Potter published another paper in *Science* magazine, which emphasised two strategies in the battle against cancer – prevention and chemotherapy, leaving out radiotherapy and surgery as 'amputative' rather than 'restorative' treatment techniques, and claiming that the sensitivity of individual cells in the development of cancer can be influenced by diet and exercise.[49]

When speaking about statistics demonstrating the increase in cancer incidence in the USA, Potter associated this rise with reduced physical activity and an increase in obesity. However, he also anticipated the objective problem (then and in the future) of the reduced 'marketplace appeal' of prevention compared to the advertising and profitability of pharmaceutical products.[50] If we add to this that in the autumn of 1946, when addressing the Omaha Section of the American Chemical Society, Potter compared the difficulties of finding a cure for cancer with finding a solution to the problem created by the invention of the atomic bomb, it may seem justified to consider his work in this period as a kind of announcement of his 'bioethical initiation'.

At the 1958 meeting of the Federation of American Societies for Experimental Biology in Philadelphia, Potter pointed out the impossibility of a single cure for cancer, since its cause is not unique. However, he anticipated the individualisation of chemotherapy. He considered oncogeny as blocked ontogeny, proving that neoplasm imitates the growth of immature tissue without reaching adult forms (which to some extent, both in terms of terminology and concept, is reminiscent of Haeckel's idea that 'ontogeny recapitulates

[48] Van Rensselaer Potter, *DNA Model Kit for Preparing – Dimensional Models of the Deoxyribonucleic Acid Double Helix According to the Watson-Crick Theory* (Minneapolis: Burgess Publishing Co., 1959).

[49] Van Rensselaer Potter, 'The role of nutrition in cancer prevention', *Science* 101, no. 2614 (1945): 105-109.

[50] Cf. Doris, 'Land-Grant Ideology', 149.

phylogeny'),[51] and compared cell resistance to drugs with the laws of evolution.[52] (Potter became closely acquainted with Darwin's work only in 1958 after purchasing a second-hand copy of the *Origin of Species*,[53] although he was actually so much under his influence that Fernando Pascual described Potter's bioethics as 'evolutionist mechanistic anthropology'.)[54] Potter's 'Minimal Deviation Hypothesis'[55] tried to establish which genetic and enzymatic alterations are important for carcinogenesis. He mentored approximately a hundred young scientists, including the future Nobel Prize winner Günter Blobel (born in 1936).[56] (James Shull recalls an anecdote when Potter did not allow Blobel to go skiing, and when the latter nevertheless did so, Potter told him not to bother returning. The teacher and the young scientist later became closer.)[57] Potter was elected to the National Academy of Sciences (1975), National Academy of Arts and Sciences, and the Wisconsin Academy of Sciences, Arts and Letters (2001),[58] and was also President of the American Society for Cell Biology (1964-5) and the American Association for Cancer Research (1974-5).

---

[51] Later, he corrected his thesis and spoke of 'partially blocked ontogeny'. Van Rensselaer Potter, 'Phenotypic diversity in experimental hepatomas: The concept of partially blocked ontogeny', *British Journal of Cancer* 38, no. 1 (1978): 1-23; Van Rensselaer Potter, 'The present status of the blocked ontogeny hypothesis of neoplasia: The thalassemia connection', *Oncodevelopmental Biology and Medicine* 2 (1981): 243-266; Van Rensselaer Potter, 'Blocked ontogeny', *Science* 28 (1987): 964; Van Rensselaer Potter, 'On the road to the blocked ontogeny theory', *Advances in Oncology* 4, no. 1 (1988): 3-8.

[52] In general, Charles Darwin was a significant inspiration for Potter, and was one of the few common sources that he shared with Fritz Jahr. Potter believed that the evidence of chemical feedback was crucial confirmation of Darwin's theory of evolution. Moreover, in disruptions to chemical feedback, Potter saw the onset of the development of cancer.

[53] Cf. Van Rensselaer Potter, 'The ethics of nature and nurture', *Zygon* 8, no. 1 (1973): 36 (3647).

[54] Fernando Pascual, 'Alcune riflessioni sulla 'bioetica' di Potter' ['Some reflections on the 'bioethics' of Potter'], *Alpha Omega* 5 (2002): 309-336.

[55] Cf. Van Rensselaer Potter, 'Recent trends in cancer biochemistry: The importance of studies on fetal tissue', *Proceedings: Canadian Cancer Conference* 8 (1969): 9-30.

[56] Born in Germany, he studied at Tübingen, and obtained his doctorate in 1967 from Madison (working there from 1962 to 1967). He received the Nobel Prize in Physiology or Medicine in 1999 for the discovery of signal peptides (the communication system of cellular proteins). From 1968, he worked at Rockefeller University in New York, and is considered a generous sponsor of the restoration of the churches and synagogues of Dresden and Leipzig. He married Laura Maioglio, the owner of the well-known, old New York Italian restaurant *Barbetta*. On hearing that Blobel had been awarded the Nobel Prize, Potter told reporters that he had immediately recognised in Blobel a man of character, and that he was not at all surprised that he had won the Nobel Prize (although there were also others at the McArdle who deserved it), and also that Blobel's brother had advised him to go to Potter to do his doctorate.

[57] James Shull, oral communication, September 2014.

[58] Cf. 'Cancer pioneer Potter dies', *The Capital Times*, 11 September 2001.

In spite of everything, Potter's contribution to science cannot be assessed easily. He was praised in the media and in the memoirs of his contemporaries, he published his works in the best journals, he received awards, and was highly esteemed. However, he missed out on the most important awards and revolutionary achievements. Potter learned from Nobel Prize winners and also corresponded with and taught some of them. For example, in April 1941, in the midst of World War Two, he corresponded with Krebs about the citric acid cycle and expressed his disagreement,[59] while in the 1950s he was in contact with Har Gobind Khorana (1922-2011), the ideator of protein synthesis, who worked first in Vancouver and then in Madison (it is possible his arrival was influenced by Potter), and who asked Potter to conduct biochemical research into ATP. James Watson (born in 1928) was allegedly also inspired in the late 1950s by Potter's ideas about the specific signalisation necessary for cell division in higher organisms,[60] and Potter definitely corresponded in 1969 with Francis Crick (1916-2004) about a 'central dogma'. This was because in Potter's time, another scientist working at the McArdle Laboratory was Howard Temin (1935-1994), who received the Nobel Prize in Physiology or Medicine in 1975 for his 'provirus hypothesis', which negated the 'central dogma' and which proved the possibility of reverse transcriptase of gene material from RNA to DNA (which Temin connected with the development of certain types of cancer, and which is today primarily connected with HIV infection). Potter also tried to convince Joshua Lederberg (1925-2008) to remain at Madison but without success. Lederberg received the Nobel Prize after leaving for Stanford in California.[61]

Today, people from Potter's laboratory still cherish his memory. The retired laboratory assistant Joyce Becker Probstein speaks about gatherings in which Potter's family also participated, and describes Potter as a person who 'knew how to take care of his people' and gladly invited them to his home and to picnics on his Portage estate. Probstein also recalls that Potter played tennis, that he would go for a ride in his car as if he was going for a walk, that he did not use computers, and that he was always well balanced.[62] (Confirmation that he did not use computers came from Potter himself in an e-mail of May 2001 in which he wrote that 'his entire internet contact is managed by very competent staff – Kristen Adler and Mary Jo Markham – who send his letters to the Network and

---

[59] McArdle Laboratory Archive, V. R. Potter, box no. 11.

[60] Van Rensselaer Potter, 'The genetic aspects of the enzyme-virus theory of cancer', *Science* 101, no. 2633 (1945): 609-610.

[61] The son of a rabbi from New Jersey, Joshua Lederberg was a molecular biologist who in 1958 won the Nobel Prize for Physiology or Medicine for the discovery that bacteria can mate and exchange genes, and was known for his research on artificial intelligence and participation in the NASA programme investigating the possibility of life on Mars. He worked in Madison from 1947 to1958.

[62] Joyce E. Becker Probstein, oral communication, September 2014.

bring him incoming messages printed on paper'.)[63] Potter's associate James Shull recalls that when Potter found out that Shull intended to adopt a child, he dedicated a lot of time and attention to seriously explaining to Shull the responsibilities of such an act. The Medical Alumni Association also highlighted Potter's merits as President of the Medical Library Building Committee.[64]

Roswell K. Boutwell (born in 1917), Professor Emeritus of Oncology, was among the first who came to the McArdle. The Boutwells played poker with the Potters, who gave their children presents such as tricycles or cradles. Potter, however, never spoke about his parents or ancestors and could not understand at all how people could waste time at work talking about private matters.[65]

Henry C. Pitot, Professor Emeritus of Oncology, Pathology and Laboratory Medicine, joined the McArdle team in 1959 and was Potter's postdoctoral student (working on hepatomas,[66] like Potter). Potter once persuaded him to eat only once in two days (dinner) and helped him find a house in Madison. Once a week, they would meet to discuss ongoing research.[67]

Richard R. Burgess, the first director of the UW Biotechnology Center, and Professor Emeritus of Oncology, who came to the McArdle in 1971, considered Potter to be a 'renaissance hero' with a broad education who was always open to new ideas. Potter offered Burgess the position of *Aldo Leopold Professor for Environmental Sciences*, but Burgess rejected this. He also recalls how Potter did not hide his emotions and began to cry when he heard that Temin had died of cancer, or that Potter would occasionally send e-mails to his acquaintances concerning an initiative or idea, such as a 'definition of life'[68] (under this title, Potter once quoted and commented on the thoughts of the Moscow oceanographer and polar explorer Pyotr Petrovich Shirshov (1905-1953) about 'complex systems' with characteristics of life).

Until recently, James Shull was head of the Department/Laboratory for eleven years. He came in 1977 from Lincoln (Nebraska) and found employment with Potter (at that time he did not know much about him but would later hear from others that he was a famous figure). He recalls that Potter called the people who Shull had stated as his referees in his presence. However, Potter later refused to

---

[63] Van Rensselaer Potter, e-mail to Anthony Cortese, dated 30 May 2001. DICEB *Fritz Jahr* Archive SuRi – IŠ – VRP 1.

[64] 'Professor of oncology Van R. Potter retires', *Wisconsin Medical Alumni Quarterly* 22, no. 3 (1982): 17.

[65] Roswell K. Boutwell, oral communication, September 2014.

[66] Cf. Van Rensselaer Potter, 'A new protocol and its rationale for the study of initiation and promotion of carcinogenesis in rat liver', *Carcinogenesis* 2, no. 12 (1981): 1375-1379.

[67] Henry C. Pitot, oral communication, September 2014.

[68] Richard Burgess, oral communication, September 2014.

mentor Shull for his PhD thesis by claiming that he was too old, and recommended to Shull a younger expert in steroid hormones. Shull described Potter as a person who stayed at work from approximately 9 in the morning until 5 in the afternoon, who read a lot, and who in particular mastered medical literature. Allegedly, he once refused the position of interim dean because he was of the opinion that somebody who is not a physician (that is, one who holds the title of PhD, like Potter, rather than MD) should not be the Dean of the Faculty of Medicine. He would not hold undergraduate courses but only taught graduate students and did not skimp on laboratory equipment either. Shull was surprised when he received from Potter a set of automatic pipettes (back where he came from, Shull had had to clean and feed the animals himself). In addition, and very atypically, Potter gave Shull permission to use the laboratory in his spare time for his own experiments. Shull recalls that Potter did not particularly care about the ethical aspects of animal testing. Potter also warned Shull about a post-doctoral student who was 'suspicious' to him. Indeed, apart from trying to avoid work, in 1981 this post-doctoral student published the results of someone else's research as his own (Potter did not succeed in withdrawing the article from the magazine in time).[69]

Paul Lambert, present Head of the Laboratory (and Department), only came to the McArdle in 1990, when Potter had already long retired. He remembers that everybody still perceived Potter as an oncologist and mostly did not understand the importance of bioethics. Potter used to question Lambert about his work, and both Lambert and Shull emphasised that they were impressed by Potter's ability to 'link what others could not or did not know how to connect'.[70]

Potter's granddaughter (and Carl's daughter) Lisa, who today lives in a small town near Philadelphia (in the mid-1990s, Potter referred to her in articles as a 'research specialist' at the McArdle), helped her grandfather in the preparation of some of his last articles (1994-1997).[71] (Potter had hired her, but often complained by asking: 'Are *you* working for *me* or am *I* working for *you*?') Lisa, who speaks Spanish and graduated in Latin American Studies and spent a year at the University of Ecuador,[72] was also present in September 2011 in Gijón, Spain, where, during the 7th World Conference on Bioethics, a plate with the name of a street dedicated to 'V. R. Potter, the father of bioethics' was unveiled.

---

[69] James Shull, oral communication, September 2014.

[70] Paul Lambert, oral communication, September 2014.

[71] Cf. Van Rensselaer Potter and Lisa Potter, 'Global Bioethics: Converting sustainable development to global survival', *Medicine and Global Survival* 2, no. 3 (1995): 185-191. This journal was published from 1991 until 2002, after which it ceased publication.

[72] Cf. *Video script for the Third National and Latin American Congress of Bioethics, President: Dr. Manuel Velasco-Suarez, Mexico City, 24-27 November, 1999, for Professor Van Rensselaer Potter, University of Wisconsin.* DICEB *Fritz Jahr* Archive SuRi – IŠ – VRP 1.

In the last period of Potter's life, his home addresses were Portage (2000) and from 1993 to 2008 Madison (Dane County). The house at 163 Prospect Avenue, the second one in Madison in which he lived (and rented rooms to students), was sold shortly after Potter's death. A walk through the forest on the Portage estate, where his son Carl lived with his wife Kathy after 1970, was a part of Potter's rehabilitation after his hip replacement. In order for Potter to enter Carl's house, a ramp had to be built. The estate originally covered 80 acres, and another 120 acres were purchased later.

During his last few years, Potter took care of his seriously ill wife Vivan, who later died in her sleep in a care centre in Middleton (a part of Madison) on 20 October 2004. She lived in the centre from 1999 and was visited by her children in the morning and by Van Rensselaer in the afternoon, who would bring her tea according to a well-established family tradition. Vivian was said to be a great swimmer and bridge player in her youth, but was later crippled by arthritis.

While he still could, Potter drove an old 1984 *Subaru* (it was his third car of the same make; he had bought his first car back in 1947) with a four-wheel drive and personalised licence plates on which was written 'YES ZPG' (*Zero Population Growth*, an organisation founded in 1968 by Paul Ehrlich and Thomas Eisner, and whose goal was to emphasise the problem of overpopulation).

Taking into consideration that Potter had three children (Leopold had had five),[73] it is not entirely clear how he imagined the population could be controlled, unless, of course, such control was intended only for specific groups of people. It is clear what Potter feared. Based on Leopold's example of deer extinction in Kaibab Forest on the edge of the Grand Canyon (the deer disappeared from the area after people exterminated the wolves which were their natural predators, which led to the uncontrolled propagation of the deer and their subsequent death from starvation), Potter anticipated the future of humankind. However, there are only a few places where Potter went into deeper consideration of this problem, mostly by weighing up the balance between freedom and necessity, citing the former World Bank leader who admired Chinese measures for limiting population growth and by recalling the old saying that 'development is the best contraceptive'.[74] (Certain modern

---

[73] This is all the more interesting given that in 1932 Leopold wrote that 'when I father more than two children I am creating an insatiable need for more printing presses, more cows, more coffee, more oil, and more rubber'. Cf. Jeff Iseminger, 'Bioethics – Brightening our lives', *Wisconsin Week*, 22 February 1989. The same in: Jeff Iseminger, 'Potter prescribes 'Global Bioethics' in Leopold tradition', *Wisconsin State Journal*, 26 February 1989.

[74] Cf. Van Rensselaer Potter, 'A response to Clements: Environmental bioethics – A call for controlled human fertility in a healthy ecosystem', *Perspectives in Biology and Medicine* 28, no. 3 (1985): 426-433.

ecologists, such as Lester Milbrath, also see overpopulation as the biggest problem of the modern world.)[75] In an interview for a newspaper,[76] Potter rejected the idea that he was in favour of forced abortion and emphasised the importance of education. He was especially against the 'macho morality' advocated by the Catholic Church or Islam, which opposed abortion and contraception in order to encourage dominance over women, nature and other people. Moreover, Potter sided with the feminist movement, quoting the book *In a Different Voice* by Carol Gilligan, a Harvard professor of pedagogy,[77] which revealed to him that women – unlike men, who are preoccupied with individual accomplishments, rights and autonomy – are more oriented towards others and the community, which was in line with Potter's idea of global ethics. Potter had read Gilligan's book for the first time in 1985. As he did with other books, he freely underlined certain sentences or even whole passages. In this book, he wrote enthusiastically: 'Women who understand women will understand and support global bioethics' on the first page, and 'Global bioethics is for women' on the inside back cover.

The last time Potter travelled outside the USA was in 1990 in the company of his son Carl, when he held a lecture on global bioethics in Trento at the invitation of the Florentine professor of anthropology Brunetto Chiarelli. He declined all later invitations and sent a video recording instead (he did this in 2001 after Ivan Šegota invited him to Lošinj; this was Potter's last video). Two years before his death, Potter published an essay in *Perspectives in Biology and Medicine,* his favourite journal, on the subject of a dignified, 'Socratic' death. For Potter, the moment when a dignified death should be chosen is the day when a person's family, doctor and social worker all agree that they don't have any other choice but to send them into a retirement home. By defending one's *personhood,* Potter suggested that 'death is not evil for an elderly person if it is voluntarily chosen and for a good reason'.[78] Potter had prepared his own obituary, dated 25 September 1997, with an empty date, age and cause of death.[79]

---

[75] Lester W. Milbrath, *Learning to Think Environmentally While There is Still Time* (Albany: State University of New York Press, 1996).

[76] George Vukelich, 'Bioethics and macho morality', *Isthmus*, 14 July 1989.

[77] Carol Gilligan, *In a Different Voice: Psychological Theory and Women's Development* (Cambridge, MA/London: Harvard University Press, 1982).

[78] Van Rensselaer Potter, 'On dying with personhood: Socratic death', *Perspectives in Biology and Medicine* 43, no. 1 (1999): 103-111.

[79] *Obituary – preview (Sept. 25, 1997), Van Rensselaer Potter II.* DICEB *Fritz Jahr* Archive SuRi – IŠ – VRP 1.

Potter died on 6 September 2001[80] at 17:20 in the arms of his granddaughter Lisa[81] of septicaemia, which had developed after a hip replacement and his refusal to take antibiotics.[82] He died five days before the September 11 attacks. Less than two hours before his death, at 15:29, he sent his 'will' to the Network, and also had a coffee and meeting scheduled with DeWitt and Lahvis for the morning of 8 September.[83] On Wednesday, 7 November 2001, at 5 in the afternoon, a commemoration was held at the Alumni Lobby in the Pyle Center in Madison. A six-page booklet was published that contained Potter's photograph and biography, quotes that Potter's sister, children and grandchildren had either written or picked out, a picture of the DNA model, and a list of 92 students who had worked in Potter's laboratory from 1948 to 1975. The commemoration programme included several of Robert Schuman's works, and addresses by Potter's children and grandchildren, Peter J. Whitehouse, and his associates Henry C. Pitot, Harris Busch and Arthur B. Pardee. The 'Memorial Resolution of the Faculty of the University of Wisconsin-Madison on the Death of Professor Emeritus Van Rensselaer Potter II' was published on 1 April 2002. It was signed by the members of the Memorial Committee – chairman Henry C. Pitot, Norman R. Drinkwater (genetics professor at the McArdle) and Charles B. Kasper (emeritus at the McArdle). In the text, Potter was described as a 'man for all seasons'.

---

[80] James E. Trosko and Henry C. Pitot, 'In memoriam: Professor Emeritus Van Rensselaer Potter II (1911-2001)', *Cancer Research* 63 (2003): 1724; Erin D. Williams, 'A legacy of bioethical sustainability: In memory of Dr. Van Rensselaer Potter II', *Global Bioethics* 14, no. 4 (2001): 49-58.

[81] Lisa Potter, e-mail to the 'Global Bioethics Network', dated 7 September 2001. DICEB *Fritz Jahr* Archive SuRi – IŠ – VRP 1.

[82] Cf. Peter J. Whitehouse, 'The rebirth of bioethics: A tribute to Van Rensselaer Potter', *Global Bioethics* 14, no. 4 (2001): 39.

[83] Calvin DeWitt, e-mail to the 'Global Bioethics Network', dated 8 September 2001. DICEB *Fritz Jahr* Archive SuRi – IŠ – VRP 1.

THE GOOD PERSON FROM WISCONSIN: V. R. POTTER IN THE CONTEXT OF SPACE AND TIME

It is not completely clear what it was that made Potter turn towards bioethics. According to what he said to Ivan Šegota in 1998,[1] he became interested in bioethical topics around 1962, when, after being invited to hold a lecture at the University of South Dakota, he decided to talk about progress.[2] In his lecture, called 'Bridge to the future: The concept of human progress',[3] Potter did not just use the term 'bridge' for the first time (upon which he later built his first 'bridge bioethics'), he also advocated 'combining an individual's knowledge of the natural sciences with knowledge of the humanities', and started to develop a concept which was later called 'acceptable survival' and for which he found confirmation in the ideas of John Platt.[4] Undoubtedly, Potter's lecture left an impression, as it was later quoted in a 1970 article in *Science* magazine by the Canadian climatologist Kenneth Hare,[5] who advocated cross-disciplinary cooperation and a broader understanding of the environment.

The relationship between the 'facts' provided by science and the 'values' suggested by theology and philosophy is one of the central issues in Potter's bioethics. Facts can be wrong or fabricated, but as a rule they still represent the system of human knowledge of nature and its possibilities. According to Potter, this knowledge should be taken into consideration when defining the values that an individual or society aspire to.[6] Only this can prevent the dominance of either scientism or philosophy, and create a bridge which allows ideas to pass in both directions.

In 1962, Potter held a speech at a ceremony which took place, among other things, to mark the 100th anniversary of the land grant to South Dakota to establish a college. After much reluctance and debate, delay and a presidential

---

[1] Šegota, 'Interviews'.

[2] For a list of Potter's works on bioethics, starting in 1962, see Williams, 'A legacy of bioethical sustainability', 55-56.

[3] Van Rensselaer Potter, 'Bridge to the future: The concept of human progress', *Land Economics* 38, no. 1 (1962): 1-8.

[4] John R. Platt, ed., *New Views on the Nature of Man* (Chicago: Chicago University Press, 1965); John R. Platt, *The Step to Man* (New York: Wiley, 1966); John R. Platt, 'What we must do', *Science* 166 (1969): 1115-1121.

[5] F. Kenneth Hare, 'How should we treat environment: University organization presently permits only piecemeal consideration of environmental problems', *Science* 167, no. 3917 (1970): 352-355.

[6] Cf. James E. Trosko, 'Scientific concepts of human nature and their implications to bioethics in a scientific and technologically-altered world', *Journal of the International Society of Bioethics* (SIBI) 9 (2003): 78-79 (68-83).

veto, the American government had used the so-called Morrill Act of 1862 (named after Congressman Justin Smith Morrill, who turned the frustration caused by his lack of formal education into state policy) to donate plots of land to federal states for the purpose of building colleges to provide education in agriculture and the mechanic arts, or to sell these plots in order to fund the construction of such colleges. This pragmatic orientation initially posed problems and resulted in courses such as 'Agricultural Greek' or 'Agricultural Philosophy',[7] but over time this orientation was interpreted in a more relaxed manner, and in the 1880s the idea was introduced to offer farmers and workers courses in history, political science and rhetoric in order to overcome their underrepresentation in politics. (The so-called Second Morrill Act was adopted in 1890, and its task was to provide the former Confederate states with money instead of land but also to impose racial equality or establish special colleges for 'persons of colour'.

As a kind of upgrading of the 'land grant' policy and educational local parochialism, the 'Wisconsin Idea' emerged. It was first formulated in 1904 by the Rector of Wisconsin University in Madison, Charles Van Hise, who asserted that he would 'never be content until the beneficent influence of the university reaches every family in the state'. This idea of the immediate 'usability' and 'territoriality' of the university ('the boundaries of the university are the boundaries of the state'; indeed, when the central university building was constructed in 1848-1849, it was located precisely one mile from the Capitol Building), which is completely different from the European tradition, is linked by some to the Protestant Social Gospel movement at the end of the 19th century.[8] That the 'Wisconsin Idea' was really just an extension of the 'land grant' philosophy was later confirmed by the Wisconsin legislative committee, which in 1858, after an analysis of the activities of the University and 'protests about the majority of what was practised there', stated that 'the population of the State of Wisconsin has an unquestionable right to demand that the University adapt to the needs of the people'.[9]

The focus of the 'land grant' philosophy and the 'Wisconsin Idea' on land, progress and communitarian awareness, and above all the fact that Potter's professional path was connected with two 'land grant' institutions – a college in South Dakota and the university in Wisconsin – led the Boston theologian Margaret E. Doris to try to build her doctoral thesis upon the idea that the key

---

[7] Vernon Carstensen, 'A century of Land-Grant colleges', *The Journal of Higher Education* 33, no. 1 (1962): 33 (30-37).

[8] For more, see Vernon Carstensen, 'The origin and early development of the Wisconsin Idea', *Wisconsin Magazine of History* 39, no. 3 (1956): 181-188; J. David Hoeveler, 'The university and the Social Gospel: The intellectual origins of the Wisconsin Idea', *Wisconsin Magazine of History* 59, no. 4 (1976): 282-298.

[9] Carstensen, 'A century of Land-Grant colleges', 32.

factors that led to the formulation of Potter's bioethics were 'land grant' and 'Wisconsin Idea' ideologies. However, the philosophical part of Doris's comprehensive thesis,[10] which she defended in April 2014 (after years of research) at the Boston University School of Theology, seems rather unconvincing, unlike its very good and useful historiographical part. Doris only read and quoted American authors and declared everything unknown to her (often European) as 'obscure'. In addition, she gave up an in-depth analytical thesis in favour of factual breadth and an abundance of information about V. R. Potter's life and work (including quotes from his works and memoirs). The title and main thesis of Doris's dissertation – 'Land-Grant Ideology, the Wisconsin Idea, and the Foundations of Van Rensselaer Potter's Bioethics' – was rather poorly backed up with arguments and, in fact, missed its mark, as there is no conclusion, and the chapters that deal with land grants and Potter are separated. However, one cannot (and should not) negate the influence of land grant ideology on Potter. This ideology cannot be used to explain everything, especially the most important issues (like Doris has attempted), but it can be used to complete the very complex mosaic of influences that directed Potter towards bioethics. (This idea, however, isn't that new. The editorial of the *Land Economics* magazine in which Potter published his South Dakota speech back in 1962 insinuated that *Potter's research was mostly carried out at a college that emerged with a land grant, and therefore emphasises the importance of such institutions*.)

That the 'Wisconsin Idea' is not really ideal for explaining Potter's work is attested to by articles in Milwaukee newspapers from 1981, when Potter received the Bristol-Myers Award. These articles ironised awarding those who dealt with pure science instead of applying it to bring more benefit to the inhabitants of Wisconsin.[11] In addition, Potter's fear of overpopulation contradicts the philosophy of land awards and the 'growth of the state in every aspect'. Did not Potter, perhaps precisely in the orientation towards technology/industry and agriculture (and the neglecting of humanism) that was typical of the land grant, see the danger of moving away from human values? In fact – and this goes against Margaret Doris's main thesis – the land grant is an idea from the primitive phase of capital accumulation that focuses on the necessity of education (although originally only in agriculture and industry), while Potter's idea of bioethics can be attributed to the mature phase in the development of a humankind which is already fearful of what has been

[10] The only publication of M. Doris connected with Potter – at least the only one that we have been able to trace – was presented at the annual meeting of the American Society for Bioethics and Humanities in 2013. Cf. Margaret Doris, 'Land-Grant ideology, the Wisconsin Idea, and the foundations of Van Rensselaer Potter's bioethics', in *American Society for Bioethics + Humanities, Annual Meeting, October 24-27, 2013, Atlanta, GA* (Atlanta: ASBH, 2013), 43.

[11] Cf. Doris, 'Land-Grant Ideology', 356.

accumulated. The same could also be said of the Wisconsin Idea, which strove to return what had been invested to the tax payers of the federal state (and was indeed pragmatic about this), while Potter strove towards opening up, globalisation and a far more abstract deliberation on survival and development. (Not to mention the fact that the mere idea that bioethics – or any other discipline – must inevitably originate from something as prosaic as land grants or the Wisconsin Idea is actually banally pragmatic.)

In any case, when speaking about the specific characteristics of Potter's time – the fear of nuclear weapons after their first and last use in Japan in 1945, the tensions of the Cold War with its occasional escalations such as the Cuban Crisis in October 1962, the sudden progress of science and medicine, the establishment and popularisation of ethical committees thanks to the Seattle haemodialysis programme in 1961-2, etc. – the influence of the individual development of Potter's intellect and his private destiny is often ignored or underestimated. Potter was a positivist who dived deeply into the basis of the process of the emergence of malignant disease (of which his grandfather and namesake had died). He was concerned about the issues of microenvironments,[12] adaptation,[13] (intracellular) communication,[14] cybernetics,[15] basic values ('dangerous knowledge', interdisciplinarity), progress (the future, control of technology), survival, evolution, and chaos (order vs. disorder). With time, Potter started projecting these questions from the cellular level to the macro-level of society (he expressly instructed his associate James Trosk about this, and Trosk allegedly had great benefit from this along his future scientific path),[16] including a comparison of ideas and DNA, and a very direct confession that his 'embarkation in bioethics arose from his cancer research activities'[17] and

---

[12] Cf. Van Rensselaer Potter, 'Intracellular responses to environmental change: The quest for optimum environment', *Environmental Research* 3, no. 2 (1970): 176-186; Van R. Potter, 'How is an optimum environment defined?' *Environmental Research* 2, no. 5 (1969): 476-487.

[13] Cf. Van Rensselaer Potter, 'Physiological adaptation at the molecular level: The frontier where research on differentiation and malignancy meet', *Perspectives in Biology and Medicine* 24, no. 4 (1981): 525-542; Van Rensselaer Potter, 'The role of the individual in modern society', in *Changing Concepts of Productive Living*, ed. Robert Dean Boyd (Madison: University of Wisconsin – University Extension, 1967), 37-51.

[14] Cf. Van Rensselaer Potter, 'Initiation and promotion in cancer formation: The importance of studies on intracellular communication', *The Yale Journal of Biology and Medicine* 53 (1980): 367-384.

[15] Cf. Van Rensselaer Potter, 'Probabilistic aspects of the human cybernetic machine', *Perspectives in Biology and Medicine* 17, no. 2 (1974): 164-183.

[16] Doris, 'Land-Grant Ideology', 315.

[17] The part of Potter's work *Global Bioethics* that provides an analogy between environmental problems and the development of cancer was later also reproduced as a chapter in a book. See Van Rensselaer Potter, 'The cancer analogy', in *Learning to Listen to the Land*, ed. Bill Willers (Washington: Island Press, 1991), 157-162.

that 'cancer is often another aspect of environmental problems'.[18] In doing so, Potter consistently tried to explain social phenomena by using formulas, algorithms and feedback diagrams, which he took from natural sciences.[19] In a memorandum from 1965, signed on behalf of an 'Interdisciplinary committee',[20] Potter consistently gave an organicistic outline of man as an information-processing machine, again by comparing processes typical of culture with genetic processes. According to Potter, modern man is in some cases exposed to a larger quantity of information than he can process, and in other cases is 'underinformed'.[21]

Judging by indirect testimonies and publications, Potter turned towards bioethical topics at least ten years earlier than he himself thought. His attention was drawn to the problem of overpopulation and loss of natural resources as early as the mid-1950s while reading Harrison Brown,[22] and this line of reflection continued with an analysis of the mutual influences of science and religion. At the end of 1957, Potter exchanged letters with the Director of the National Institutes of Health (NIH), James Shannon (1904-1994), complaining that science was moving away from society. After that, he formed a group that launched an 'Interdisciplinary Seminar on the Future of Man'. The management of the University of Wisconsin contacted Potter's Committee for Interdisciplinary Research on the Future of Man in 1967, asking for answers about the purpose of higher education, the goals of the university and its constituent parts, and the role of students and their organisations. Potter's Committee provided an answer in accordance with his ideas about knowledge and wisdom, also taking into consideration Margaret Mead's theses.[23] However, the Committee was soon dismissed and replaced by the Institute for Environmental Studies led by a member of Potter's committee who had different ideas.[24] In September 1962, Potter, based on his experience with the Seminar, submitted a proposal for the establishment of an Institute for Integrated Studies in Science and the Humanities (very similar to today's concept of integrative

---

[18] 'Know your Madisonian: Van R. Potter', *Wisconsin State Journal*, 19 December 1972.

[19] Van Rensselaer Potter, *Bioetika: most prema budućnosti* [*Bioethics: Bridge to the Future*], translated by Ines Radinović (Rijeka: Katedra za društvene znanosti Medicinskog fakulteta u Rijeci / Hrvatsko društvo za kliničku bioetiku / Hrvatsko bioetičko društvo / Međunarodno udruženje za kliničku bioetiku, 2007), 227-238.

[20] Probably 'Interdisciplinary seminar on the future of man', which he presented.

[21] Van Rensselaer Potter, 'Man as an information-processing machine', manuscript dated 13 January 1965. McArdle Laboratory Archive, V. R. Potter.

[22] Harrison Brown, *The Challenge of Man's Future* (New York: Viking Press, 1954). Potter mentions in one place that he read Brown shortly after returning from Peru.

[23] Cf. V. R. Potter, D. A. Baerreis, R. A. Bryson, J. W. Curvin, G. Johansen, J. McLeod, J. Rankin and K. R. Symon, 'Purpose and function of the university', *Science* 167, no. 3925 (1970): 1590-1593.

[24] Cf. Doris, 'Land-Grant Ideology', 242.

bioethics), in which he advocated the broadening of horizons instead of 'superspecialisation' (building on the legacy of Leopold).[25] The institute would have a historical approach but not methodological, as it would give recommendations and be set up as a post-graduate training centre.[26]

In November 1958, Potter prepared a lecture at the University (No. 18) on the topic of 'Human progress with respect to knowledge of nucleic acid function', in which he talked about three concepts of progress: religious (knowledge of God's will, preparation for the afterlife, and the ethical variant of the Golden Rule), materialistic (an increase in material well-being and the Darwinian concept of 'survival of the fittest'), and Neo-Darwinist or scientific (a sophisticated interpretation of the 'survival of the fittest', short-term natural selection that leads to extermination). The lecture ended with the relationship between science, scientists, and ethics. The diagrams that followed the outline of the lecture put the emphasis on the feedback relationships in ignorance vs. competence and 'crude environment' vs. 'controlled environment'. A special graph shows that a golden era of civilisation is achieved when competence and control are at their highest level and in line with needs. Later, needs grow and competence and control decline, which consequently leads to the collapse of civilisation.[27]

In the early 1960s, Potter was one of the scientists who signed a series of petitions calling for the renunciation of the nuclear weapons programme. In 1964, he published an article in *Science* magazine in which he asked 'can science aid in the search for sophistication in dealing with order and disorder in human affairs'?[28] The article reveals Potter's concern about 'dangerous knowledge' that can lead to scandals like the ones with thalidomide or pesticide poisoning. According to Potter, 'science is not wisdom, but we can use the scientific method to seek wisdom'. New science must be combined with old wisdom (humanities), and wisdom should be defined as 'knowledge on how to use knowledge to improve the human condition'. Potter's understanding of the idea as the fundamental unit of cultural information, i.e. 'cultural DNA', attracted the attention of Carl P. Swanson (1910-1996), the editor of Potter's future book, who would also influence Rachel Carson.[29] As early as February 1965, Potter published a similar essay in the *Nation* magazine entitled 'Council on the future',

---

[25] Cf. Van Rensselaer Potter, *Global Bioethics: Building on the Leopold Legacy* (East Lansing, MI: Michigan State University Press, 1988), 15.

[26] Van Rensselaer Potter, 'Memorandum: A proposal for an Institute for Integrated Studies in Science and the Humanities', manuscript dated 14 September 1962. McArdle Laboratory Archive, V. R. Potter.

[27] McArdle Laboratory Archive, V. R. Potter, box no. 11.

[28] Van Rensselaer Potter, 'Society and science: Can science aid in the search for sophistication in dealing with order and disorder in human affairs?' *Science* 146, no. 3647 (1964): 1018-1022.

[29] Ibid.

which was aimed at a wider and non-scientific readership. By emphasising the already well-known thesis about 'dangerous knowledge', Potter this time focused on the responsibilities of scientists towards society and the gap between those who *know* (scientists) and those who *use* (technologists, as Potter calls them). By criticising the reliance of American culture on pragmatism ('if something is doable and makes a profit, let's do it'), Potter, actually spoke about the pressure on scientists and called for something that would later become known – and accepted in Europe – as the precautionary principle. For Potter, the danger of new knowledge lies in its application, and the task of politicians is to act strongly to secure monitoring over technology. In his often utopian spirit of an amiable ambitious fantasist, Potter proposed establishing a fourth branch of the federal government (in addition to the legislative, executive and judicial) – the 'Council on the Future', which would gather scientists from natural and humanistic areas, which would have an advisory role and a legislative initiative, and which would deliberate on the most important fields of scientific research. Entering the sphere of real politics, Potter criticised the existing dualist system in which one group penalises the other and described the conservatives as 'pragmatists thinking only of the present', and liberals as 'pragmatists thinking only of the future'. According to Potter, syncretism would demand a realism which calls for knowledge about both 'the things we know and the things we don't know'.[30] At a conference in 1972, Potter used the term 'bioethics' to explain his ideas about social responsibility and formulated his Bioethical Credo in 6 points that emphasise beliefs and commitment.[31] During the first seven months of 1973, Potter participated at a Leonardo's seminar (outside the McArdle and cancer research), developing his own bioethical ideas together with other University professors.

In February 1966, in a letter to Robben W. Fleming, Chancellor of the University of Wisconsin, Potter tried to outline the underlying philosophy of the University's 'new college', which should take into account the then ongoing discussion at Harvard about the need to return general content to college education. According to Potter, in the first two years of study such content from the natural and socio-humanistic sciences should represent 80%, and specialised content only 20%. Potter also spoke about the need to bring technical innovation into classroom teaching, and moving the campus to a new location, etc.[32]

In September 1968, at the Swiss Château de Bossey near Lake Geneva, Potter participated (together with people such as Edmund Pellegrino) at a meeting

---

[30] Van Rensselaer Potter, 'Council on the future', *Nation*, 8 February 1965.

[31] Van Rensselaer Potter, 'Bioethics for whom?', *Annals of the New York Academy of Sciences* 196 (1972): 204 (200-205).

[32] Van Rensselaer Potter, 'Basic philosophy for UW 'New College' – 1st draft report to Chancellor Fleming', manuscript dated 28 February 1966. McArdle Laboratory Archive, V. R. Potter.

('consultations') organised by the local Ecumenical Institute, and led a group that revised the Helsinki Declaration of 1964. Although Potter's group proposed very concrete positions about trials involving humans and the role of science in society, the report was not officially adopted (and nor was any other from the conference).[33]

Potter's 'invention' of bioethics in the terminological sense happened in the first half of 1970. Judging by his correspondence with his publishers, it turns out that the first articles that use the name of the new discipline are actually chapters of a finished manuscript that was later published as a book (*Bioethics: Bridge to the Future*). It is interesting that Potter tried to speed up the publication of the chapters/articles in the *Perspectives in Biology and Medicine* journal, as if he was afraid that someone would steal his idea (which actually happened in the end, as we know). Moreover, he consulted a member of the editorial board, Harold Rusch, with whom he worked at the McArdle, and who, allegedly, had even persuaded Potter to write the article for this journal. Of course, Potter's hurry can also be interpreted as a fear that someone else would launch the term, which is actually not so original (not to mention the fact that it was already known more than four decades earlier). The first chapter of what would later be a book was published in the *Perspectives in Biology and Medicine* journal without being reviewed.[34]

At *Bellarmine* Catholic College (*Bellarmine* University since 2000) in Louisville, Kentucky, a panel on 'American ethics' was held in 1974. On this panel, the doctors John P. Bell, David H. Bizot and William P. VonderHaar, together with chemist Paul L. Corio discussed Potter's introductory lecture on the subject of 'Humility – with responsibility – is the first rule of American professional ethics'. One of the more interesting remarks was definitely the one by VonderHaar, stating that just 'as it is difficult to be a politician and remain honest, so it is difficult to stay in medicine and remain ethical'.[35]

After assuming the leading position in the American Association for Cancer Research, Potter tried to take advantage of it in order to impose the subject of '(bio)ethics for oncologists', especially in the light of the then controversy about the carcinogenicity of tobacco smoke and tar. In his 'presidential address' in 1975, he pledged a combination of humility and responsibility as a logical consequence of admitting fallibility[36] (to the general disappointment of his

[33] For more on this, see Doris, 'Land-Grant Ideology', 226-236.

[34] Cf. Doris, 'Land-Grant Ideology', 254.

[35] Jessica M. Daniels, 'In ethics professionals need education', *The Record*, 31 January 1974.

[36] Van Rensselaer Potter, 'Humility with responsibility: A bioethic for oncologists', *Cancer Research* 35 (1975): 2297-2306. Margaret Doris states that there is no transcript of Potter's address (Doris, 'Land-Grant Ideology', 342), but this is not true. A transcript with the same

colleagues in the audience who were expecting to hear about the results of Potter's experiments).

Drawing on the thoughts of Garrett Hardin and Aldo Leopold, Potter sketched the five stages of the development of environmental bioethics in 1977: 1) environmental damage becomes apparent to Leopold's 'average individual', and moral indignation arises; 2) knowledge of the problems and their extent, including 'new or intriguing ecological situations' becomes a new discipline; 3) moral indignation requires preventive and creative countermeasures; 4) moral pressure and factual information result in bioethical guidelines; and 5) moral pressure transforms bioethical guidelines into legal sanctions, that is, 'mutual coercion which is jointly agreed upon'.[37] In our time, environmental bioethics is experiencing a resurgence, which is not so unexpected, as it is being intriguingly coordinated: from the activities of the Hastings Center and the initiative of Peter Whitehouse, to the issue of the Italian journal *Studia Bioethica* dedicated to the subject of *Bioetica ed ecologia umana* (year 8, issue 2, 2015),[38] the *Environmental Ethics* textbook by Andreas Brenner, [39] and the recalling of Potter's 'unifying' reflections in the work of Gruen and Ruddick.[40] It would seem that both in Europe and in the USA, a wave of interest has been generated to spread bioethical visions. (There are also those who try to emphasise the difference between bioethics and environmental ethics, albeit without much success.)[41]

There is no doubt that Potter was always and to a great extent (sometimes even uncritically) influenced by what he was reading. Unlike certain short-term influences, some authors became and remained permanent sources of inspiration to Potter, especially Rachel Carson, Margaret Mead, Aldo Leopold, Pierre Teilhard de Chardin and Albert Schweitzer.

---

title and subtitle '*Presidential Address: Am. Assoc. for Cancer Research, Thursday, May 8, 1975. San Diego, Calif.*' exists in the McArdle Laboratory Archive, V. R. Potter.

[37] Van Rensselaer Potter, 'Introduction: Evolving ethical concepts', *BioScience* 27, no. 4 (1977): 251-253.

[38] Rivista della Facoltà di Bioetica, Ateneo Pontificio *Regina Apostolorum*, Roma.

[39] Andreas Brenner, *Umweltethik: ein Lehr- und Lesebuch* [*Environmental Ethics: A Textbook and a Reader*] (Würzburg: Königshausen & Neumann, 2014).

[40] Lori Gruen and William Ruddick, 'Biomedical and environmental ethics alliance: Common causes and grounds', *Bioethical Inquiry* 6 (2009): 457-466.

[41] Cf. Giovanni Russo, 'Storia della bioetica dalle origini ad oggi' ['The history of bioethics from its origins to the present'], in *Storia della bioetica: le origini, il significato, le istituzioni* [*The History of Bioethics: Origins, Significance and Institutions*], ed. Giovanni Russo (Roma: Armando Editore, 1995), 19 (7-99).

The oceanologist Rachel Carson (1907-1964) attracted the most attention with her book *Silent Spring*,[42] dedicated to Albert Schweitzer, in which she pointed out the fatal toxicity of pesticides (especially DDT). Carson's book, published in 1962,[43] was not only declared 'book of the month' but was also published as a series of articles in *The New Yorker*. Its author, then already undergoing radiotherapy due to breast cancer, was accused by advocates of the chemical industry of being 'attractive and single, and therefore obviously a communist'.

The anthropologist Margaret Mead (1901-1978) influenced Potter with her book on continuities in cultural evolution,[44] and even more with her earlier article on her vision of university[45] (Potter later confessed that this article was the trigger for his own spiritual transformation). In this article, Margaret Mead seeks to bring her anthropology closer to the natural sciences, emphasising the significance of utopia in our culture (including heaven, hell, communism, etc.), and three sources of 'more vivid' utopias that we should turn to: children's imagination, ethnographic data about other cultures, and scientific discoveries. According to Mead, universities need *Chairs of the Future*, chairs for those who will devote themselves, with all the necessary scholarship and attention, to developing science to the full extent of its possibilities for the future. Potter met M. Mead in person in 1959 during a lunch in Boston, and later remembered her clarity and persuasiveness that 'there are those who strive to divide and see differences in everything (*splitters*), and others who, like her, strive to unite, always looking for similarities (*lumpers*).'

Of course, the person who had the crucial influence on Potter's bioethical ideas – as acknowledged by Potter himself – was Aldo Leopold. A son of German immigrants (they spoke German at home) Clare Starker and carpenter Carl Leopold, Aldo Leopold (born in Burlington in Iowa in 1887 – died in Baraboo in Wisconsin in 1948) was raised in the environmentalist spirit, which included planting an oak whenever a child was born in the house. At the age of 11, he used to watch birds closely (but also kill a lot of crows), hunted and fished 'considerately' (?) with his father,[46] and in 1909 graduated from the Yale School

---

[42] The fiftieth anniversary of the publication of this book in 2012 was marked by a number of commemorative events. As a result of a joint initiative by Ludwig-Maximilian University and the Deutsches Museum, and with the support of the German Federal Ministry of Education and Research, the Rachel Carson Centre for Environment and Study was opened in Munich in 2009 (cf. http://www.carsoncenter.uni-muenchen.de/index.html).

[43] Rachel Carson, *Silent Spring* (Boston/London: Houghton Mifflin / Penguin Books, 1962-2000).

[44] Margaret Mead, *Continuities in Cultural Evolution* (New Haven, CT: Yale University Press, 1964).

[45] Margaret Mead, 'Towards more vivid utopias', *Science* 126, no. 3280 (1957): 957-961.

[46] This reminds us of the ambiguous reputation of Theodore Roosevelt as a hunter but also as a saviour of bears (*Teddy Bear*) and a lover and protector of nature.

of Forestry as a student and follower of Gifford Pinchot, forestry pioneer and friend of T. Roosevelt (who, admittedly, had the opportunistic attitude that nature should be used 'reasonably'). His career took Aldo Leopold to the Forest Service in Arizona and New Mexico, and in 1924 he moved to Madison. In 1933, Leopold published a textbook on fauna management and was appointed Professor of Game Management in the Agricultural Economics Department (the first one in the USA), and in 1935 the Leopold family (Aldo Leopold married his cousin Estella Bergere) started an experiment to ecologically restore a run-down farm near Baraboo (Wisconsin) by planting pines and trying to preserve the prairie. In April 1948, Leopold succumbed to a heart attack on this very farm while trying to put out a fire that had hit his neighbour's lawn. Even though he had received recognition for his work during his lifetime (in 1947 he was appointed President of the Ecological Society of America),[47] it was a year after his death that Oxford University Press published his influential book *A Sand County Almanac*.[48] This book is a kind of diary in which Leopold described the natural changes from month to month that he observed from his Wisconsin hut, led by the thought that 'we grieve only for what we know'.[49] When formulating his *land ethic*, Leopold defined 'land' as 'not merely soil; it is a fountain of energy flowing through a circuit of soils, plants, and animals',[50] and saw nature as a 'biotic pyramid' which rests on natural species and which resists human interventions with more or less strength and success.

Aldo Leopold's influence on Potter is obvious and explicit. Potter dedicated his first book (on bridge bioethics) to Leopold, and added the subtitle 'Building on the Leopold Legacy' to his second one (on global bioethics). Even in his private life, Potter followed Leopold's example. In 1935, Leopold had bought a farm by the Wisconsin River and started using a renovated chicken coop called the *Shack* with his family during the weekends. Here is where Leopold, while suffering from trigeminal neuralgia, devised his laboratory of 'ideas' and actions aimed at restoring nature. Around 1962, Van Rensselaer Potter chose a piece of land together with his son Toby (they even rented an airplane so they could inspect the terrain from above) not far from Portage (Portage was the home of John Muir and his family), 60 km north of Madison, and in 1971 built a small cottage so he could think and write there (Arne Næss, founder of the Deep Ecology studied by Potter, also had a similar practice). Potter called his cottage *Stuga*, a

[47] Cf. Curt Meine, 'Aldo Leopold: Connecting conservation science, ethics, policy, and practice', in *Linking Ecology and Ethics for a Changing World: Values, Philosophy, and Action*, eds. R. Rozzi, S. T. A. Pickett, C. Palmer, J. J. Arnesto and J. B. Callicott (Dordrecht: Springer, 2013), 173-184.

[48] Curt Meine, *Aldo Leopold: His Life and Work* (Madison: University of Wisconsin Press, 1988). A collection of Leopold's essays entitled *Round River*, was also published posthumously, thanks to Luna, Aldo's daughter.

[49] Aldo Leopold, *A Sand County Almanac* (New York. Ballantine Books, 1949-1970), 52.

[50] Ibid, 253.

Swedish word for a cottage (Potter lived in Sweden from 1938 to 1940, and his mother-in-law was of Swedish descent). *Stuga* obtained an annexe in 1981 when Potter brought an iron tower with a windmill from an abandoned farm which he would climb to fix the propeller on each time it was knocked down by the wind. *Stuga* had solar panels installed and most of the furniture was made by Potter. The stove ran on gas, and igniting the fire was Potter's favourite 'job'. The original idea was to build *Stuga* on the highest point of the estate (which can be seen with the naked eye from the highest floor of the McArdle), but Potter later changed this location to the present one and called it Shangri-La after the literary and mythical Himalayan paradise.

This practical Leopold-Potterian 'farm bioethics' was later adopted by others like Calvin DeWitt, who worked together with Potter on the establishment of the University of Wisconsin Center for Bioethical Sustainability.[51] Enthralled by Protestant ethics and religion, DeWitt imposed a sort of stewardship which involved the restoration and regeneration of prairies, forests and waters while running the town of Dunn in the 1970s.[52]

The extent of the impact of Leopold's *A Sand County Almanac* [53] on Potter can be seen from the testimony of James Trosko, who immediately after joining Potter in 1972 was given the *Almanac* to read. Later on, Potter even took him to 'a place north of Madison where Leopold had started writing his book'.[54] Unlike Potter's ideas, Aldo Leopold's were accepted across the USA. Leopold argued that we were all 'participants in two great experiments: one is based on the assumption that the preservation of nature is something that people can buy, and the other one assumes that it is something that people have to learn how to do properly', and therefore advocated research that would improve education - both professional and general.[55] In 1982, Leopold's children founded the Aldo Leopold Foundation, which manages the farm in Baraboo and the copyright of his book. In 2004, the Governor of Wisconsin declared the first weekend of March as Aldo Leopold Weekend throughout the entire federal state territory.[56] Since 1911, Wisconsin has had the Wisconsin State Forest Nursery, and the University also has an arboretum. Obviously, not everyone supported Leopold's 'land ethics'. The philosophers John Passmore and Richard Watson, as well as the animal rights

---

[51] Cf. Peter J. Whitehouse, 'Van Rensselaer Potter: An intellectual memoir', *Cambridge Quarterly of Healthcare Ethics* 11 (2002): 333 (331-334).

[52] Cf. http://faculty.nelson.wisc.edu/dewitt/

[53] 'Sand counties' is the name that Leopold used for several counties in Wisconsin.

[54] Doris, 'Land-Grant Ideology', 314.

[55] Cf. Meine, *Aldo Leopold*, 370-373.

[56] Cf. www.aldoleopold.org

theorist Tom Regan, thought that biocentric concepts like Leopold's jeopardised human rights and led to totalitarianism or even 'environmental fascism'.[57]

The Jesuit, palaeontologist and philosopher Pierre Teilhard de Chardin (1881-1955), an 'environmental theologian',[58] was close to Potter because of his endeavour to reconcile science and religion, and Schweitzer because of his differentiation between science, knowledge, and wisdom. Teilhard de Chardin, a native Frenchman who lived in England, Egypt and China, and who then settled in the USA, was a Vatican renegade for most of his life, known for his original combination of evolutionary and Christian doctrines. According to Teilhard, consciousness is evolving and requires unity ('unanimisation'), with the final goal being the 'Omega Point', which is God.[59] Potter knew both de Chardin's books, and also wrote a review of *The Future of Man*.[60]

The doctor, philosopher, theologian, musician and Nobel Prize winner Albert Schweitzer (1875-1965) asserted that we must be pessimistic due to our experience, but also hopeful in accordance with our faith. He also concluded that 'our time has revealed how to separate knowledge from opinion, with the consequence that we really have free science but not a science that contemplates'.[61]

Among the thinkers who must have influenced Potter – not directly or decisively (Potter never mentioned Muir in his two books about bioethics, but mentioned him in at least one of his articles as a pioneer of environmental bioethics)[62] but indirectly via Leopold and by other means – was John Muir (1838-1914), a travel writer who travelled through the American wilderness, discovering a glacier in Alaska. He was a 'conservationist' (or conservation philosopher),[63] as

---

[57] Cf. George Sessions, '1984: A postscript', in *Deep Ecology: Living as if Nature Mattered*, eds. Bill Devall and George Sessions (Salt Lake City/Layton: Gibbs M. Smith, Inc. / Peregrine Smith Books, 1985), 254 (254-256).

[58] Simone Morandini, *Teologija i ekologija* [*Theology and Ecology*], translated by Slavko Antunović (Zagreb: Kršćanska sadašnjost, 2013), 24.

[59] Cf. Pierre Teilhard de Chardin, *The Phenomenon of Man*, translated by Bernard Wall (London/New York: Wm. Collins Sons & Co., Ltd. / Harper & Brothers, 1959); Pierre Teilhard de Chardin, *The Future of Man*, translated by Norman Denny (London/New York: Wm. Collins Sons & Co., Ltd. / Harper & Row, Publishers, 1964).

[60] Van Rensselaer Potter, 'Teilhard de Chardin and the concept of purpose', *Zygon* 3, no. 4 (1968): 367-376.

[61] Albert Schweitzer, *An Anthology*, translated by Charles R. Joy (Boston: Beacon, 1947), 47.

[62] Van Rensselaer Potter, 'Bioethics and the human prospect', in *The Culture of Biomedicine, Studies in Science and Culture*, vol. 1, eds. Heyward Brock and Ann Harward (Newark/London/ Toronto: University of Delaware Press / Associated University Press, 1984), 130-131 (124-137).

[63] Although he does not talk about Muir, for more on the history of conservation ideas, biodiversity, etc., see Curt Meine, 'Biodiversity conservation', in *Bioethics* (*Encyclopedia of Bioethics*), 4th edition, ed. Bruce Jennings (Farmington Hills: Macmillan Reference USA,

they are known in the USA (he wanted to build a place in Wisconsin where future generations could see the plants from the time of the colonisation of the American West), who convinced the American president Theodore Roosevelt in 1903 of the necessity of a national programme for the conservation of natural resources and successfully fought for a special status for the Grand Canyon and other areas. 'The clearest way into the Universe is through a forest wilderness'; 'In God's wildness lies the hope of the world'; 'The mountains are fountains of men as well as of rivers, of glaciers, of fertile soil' are just a few of Muir's thoughts. The one that brings him closest to Jahr is the idea that nature should be preserved not only for humans but for itself (he is known for his attitude that even rattlesnakes should be preserved, because otherwise, if we adopt the opinion that everything that humans find detestable and useless must be destroyed, then we consider ourselves gods). Even though Potter and Muir could not have met in person (Potter was three years old when Muir died), the life of John Muir was closely connected to Wisconsin. A Scot by birth, he moved to the Fox River not far from Portage in Wisconsin as an 11-year-old boy with his family. Moreover, he attended the University of Madison, but changed this place of 'hungry and happy days full of hope' for the *University of the Wilderness*. He did not obtain a degree until 1897, when he was awarded an honorary doctorate in law by the University of Madison.[64] Muir was greatly influenced by Waldo Emerson. He read his works, and was influenced by his Greek and Latin professor, Emerson's friend James Davie Butler, and met him in Yosemite in 1871.

In the foreword to his 1988 book on global bioethics,[65] Potter, apart from quoting Mead, emphasised the particular impact that two people had had on him: the British developmental biologist and animal geneticist (and Marxist) Conrad Hal Waddington (1905-1975),[66] who advocated that each generation should develop its own ethics as a kind of 'contemporary discipline' ('biological wisdom'; 'supra-ethics'; 'an ethical system of general values'), which would

---

2014). For an interpretation of Potter's global bioethics in the light of biodiversity, see Marianna Gensabella, 'Biodiversity and the Global Bioethics of Van Rensselaer Potter', in *Proceedings of the 1st EMUNI Research Souk 2009 (EMUNI ReS 2009): The Euro-Mediterranean Student Research Multi-Conference* (Messina: Università degli Studi di Messina, 2009), 1-13.

[64] Edwin Way Teale, ed., *The Wilderness World of John Muir* (Boston/New York: Mariner Books, 1954-2001), 60-72.

[65] Potter, *Global Bioethics*, 2-4.

[66] Cf. Conrad H. Waddington, *The Ethical Animal* (Chicago: University of Chicago Press, 1967). Waddington suggests the term 'epigenotype' for the complex development process between genotypes and phenotypes (cf. C. H. Waddington, 'The epigenotype', *Endeavour*, January 1942, 18-20), o 'epigenetic' for a combination of epigenesis and genetics (cf. Linda van Speybroeck, 'From epigenesis to epigentics: The case of C. H. Waddington', *Annual of the New York Academy of Sciences* 981 (2002): 61-81).

reflect the problems of its times, and Theodosius Dobzhansky (1900-1975), an American evolutionist of Ukrainian descent, who, even though he declared himself as Orthodox, criticised the religious insistence on creationism (close to the attitudes and language of Teilhard de Chardin),[67] and who taught Potter that there is no biological law which would guarantee prosperity, including the survival of humankind, and that this 'natural disadvantage' can only be overcome by a united human intellect.[68]

There are some sources that Potter never mentioned, but which might have had an even greater influence on the development of his bioethical thought than those mentioned. At the 41st annual meeting of the South Dakota Academy of Science, in the spring of 1956, Potter probably heard (or read later on) the lecture of the President of the Academy, Frank W. Jobes, who spoke about the dangers of the American civilisational habit of 'putting all one's eggs in one basket', that is, turning towards science at the expense of the humanities and ethics.[69] It comes as no surprise that just a few months later, in the autumn of that same year, (*post hoc, ergo propter hoc*?), Potter outlined the main direction of his own bioethical credo in the editorial of the *Cancer Research* journal, i.e. that the growth of the quantum of knowledge, associated with the pressure to produce, publish and find sources of financing, brings scientists into a situation in which they no longer use their creative thinking or grow with the content of their knowledge. In doing so, Potter, starting from a seemingly banal laboratory daily routine, actually raises the key issue of (his own and general) future bioethics: to bridge the road from almost mechanical knowledge to long-term cultural wisdom. Potter even offered a solution. He advocated the forming of groups of four scientists (*Advanced Study Groups*) who would not have to worry about their existence (scholarship 1 + 1 year), and whose only task would be to discuss and 'organise' certain areas of knowledge as a starting point for their own studies, which would encompass as many related fields as possible. This would be a long-term project that would yield results after five to ten years. (Potter went so far as to suggest that, when selecting candidates for such groups, one should also take into account the character of a candidate's wife in order to avoid the disastrous impact of 'women who prefer personal gain over science', and grant the project participants long-distance phone calls and flexible working hours, etc.)[70]

---

[67] Theodosius Dobzhansky, 'Nothing in biology makes sense except in the light of evolution', *American Biology Teacher* 35 (1973): 125-129.

[68] Theodosius Dobzhansky, 'Evolution at work', *Science* 127, no. 3306 (1958): 1091-1098; Theodosius Dobzhansky, *Genetics and the Origin of Species* (New York: Columbia University Press, 1937).

[69] Cf. Doris, 'Land-Grant Ideology', 160-162.

[70] Van Rensselaer Potter, 'A plea for formal support for study and reflection', *Cancer Research* 16, no. 8 (1956): 725-727.

Connecting the ideas of different authors might make them seem less original, but it definitely makes them stronger and also complements them mutually. The first notion that this idea of Potter's is reminiscent of is that of Fritz Jahr (whom we assume Potter did not know about) and his commitment to reforming school education and the taking into account of different views in the consideration of important issues (*Gesinnungseinstellungen*).[71] Another similarity – and a less accidental one – connects Potter's initiative with a lecture by Margaret Mead held in December 1956 (and published in *Science* magazine a year later). In her lecture, Mead advocated the establishment of 'chairs of the future' at universities, which would reduce the differences between artistic and humanistic views on the one hand and scientific and technological ones on the other. Finally, in Potter's article we can also identify a similarity with the later concept of pluri-perspective comprehension of bioethical topics which results in orientation knowledge, as well as the interesting idea that bioethics is generally conceived to shape public discussion or dialogue, which means that the public can count on bioethicists to represent the public interest.[72]

In his pioneering bioethical works, the articles that used the word bioethics for the first time since 1938: 'Bioethics: The science of survival',[73] 'Biocybernetics and survival',[74] and 'Disorder as a built-in component of biological systems: The survival imperative'[75] (here we can't help but remember Jahr's 'bioethical imperative'), and the book *Bioethics: Bridge to the Future*,[76] Potter deplored the dehumanisation of science and the fact that rapid modern technological and medical advancements brought knowledge but not the wisdom how to use this knowledge properly. According to Potter, re-establishing an ecological balance[77] and the protection of natural resources could only be guaranteed by a new science that he called 'bioethics' (deriving this term from 'biological science' and 'ethics', that is, returning lost moral values to biology), which he saw as a

[71] Cf. Iva Rinčić and Amir Muzur, 'Od bioetičara-učenika do bioetičara-učitelja: pijetizam i edukacija u životu i djelu Fritza Jahra' ['From bioethicist student to bioethicist teacher: Pietism and education in the life and work of Fritz Jahr'], *Jahr* 3, no. 5 (2012): 111-116.

[72] Cf. John H. Evans, *The History and Future of Bioethics: A Sociological View* (New York: Oxford University Press, 2012), 77.

[73] Van Rensselaer Potter, 'Bioethics: The science of survival', *Perspectives in Biology and Medicine* 14 (1970): 127-153.

[74] Van Rensselaer Potter, 'Biocybernetics and survival', *Zygon* 5, no. 3 (1970): 229-246.

[75] Van Rensselaer Potter, 'Disorder as a built in component of biological systems: The survival imperative', *Zygon* 6, no. 2 (1971): 135-150.

[76] Van Rensselaer Potter, *Bioethics: Bridge to the Future* (Englewood Cliffs, NJ: Prentice-Hall, Inc., 1971).

[77] In order to better understand the time and avant-garde quality of Potter's appeal, it is necessary to recall the humorous remark of William Milstead, who on the appearance of Potter's first book said that first of all 'we need to show that ecology is science and not hysteria'. William W. Milstead, 'Review: Bioethics – Bridge to the Future by Van Rensselaer Potter', *American Biology Teacher* 33, no. 9 (1971): 560-561.

'bridge' between natural and human sciences. The misunderstanding about defining the tasks of bioethics and the expectations of this discipline was partly caused by the fact that its name was logically-epistemologically and linguistically-terminologically incorrectly coined. This discrepancy between philosophy and practice is not present in Jahr, who derived the term bioethics in the classical way from 'bios' and 'ethos '.[78] Further confusion concerning Potter's first book was caused by his distinctive style. As Henk ten Have has correctly observed in his recent study, the connection between chapters is not always obvious, and the text is an eclectic mixture of components of different theories and authors, which consequently results in a rather poor visionary quality. Potter's mosaic style, in Henk ten Have's opinion, is not the result of an analytical way of solving problems, but of attempts and patching.[79] According to written testimony by Potter's close associate, geneticist James Trosko (born in 1938), addressed to Margaret Doris, Potter had the information that Prentice Hall, publisher of his book, had decided to discontinue publication because the feedback that they received from over 900 universities and colleges that used his book, was predominately negative reviews.[80] (Confirmation of this is the later decision of this publishing house not to publish Potter's new book on global bioethics at all). Another characteristic of Potter's style could have resulted in mistrust on the part of the readership, especially the scientific part. Potter was inclined to read and interpret in a way that supported his theory to such extent that he would go as far as to distort the original idea. This was noticed by Curt Meine, Leopold's biographer and certainly the leading authority on him, in Potter's reading of Aldo Leopold, as Potter found arguments in favour of his own global bioethics in Leopold's works.[81] In his approach to the neural fabric of morality, Potter was naively enthusiastic about the case of Phineas Gage (a 19th-century railway worker who survived a serious accident) and simplified the case to such an extent that he spoke about the 'genes for morality that were pulled from Gage's brain'.[82]

For complex ideas such as Potter's, it is logical to seek inspiration in his immediate material and spiritual surroundings of Wisconsin. If someone lives and works for a long period of time surrounded by a certain tradition, it can be expected that this tradition, directly or indirectly, will affect his or her ideas. The native inhabitants of Wisconsin – the Ojibwe, Menominee, and other tribes –

[78] See the detailed discussion on the prefix 'bio' in Iva Rinčić and Amir Muzur, *Fritz Jahr i rađanje europske bioetike* [*Fritz Jahr and the Emergence of European Bioethics*] (Zagreb: Pergamena, 2012), 143-152.

[79] ten Have, 'Potter's notion of bioethics'.

[80] Doris, 'Land-Grant Ideology', 313.

[81] Curt Meine, 'Van Rensselaer Potter: Global Bioethics: Building on the Leopold Legacy', *Environmental Ethics* 11, no. 3 (1989): 281-285.

[82] Van Rensselaer Potter, 'Global Bioethics: Linking genes to ethical behavior', *Perspectives in Biology and Medicine* 39, no. 1 (1995): 118-131.

could rightly be called 'proto-ecologists' (or 'environmental warriors', as they call themselves), for not only do they follow the 'seventh generation philosophy' (which requires that we think how our actions will affect seven generations into the future), which brings them close to the 'precautionary principle', but they also very actively struggle for the preservation of natural resources. In the 1960s, Hilary Waukau secured abundant financing for the *Nature Awareness and Cultural Center* on the Wolf River; in the mid-1970s, the United Tribes successfully blocked the bulldozing of Native American mounds at Camp Wakanda (in the words of Walter Bresette, 'Our beings, like the growing trees, are rooted in the mounds')[83] and also the mining of the *Exxon Minerals* company; in 1986, the *Lake Superior Greens* political party was established (later renamed *Wisconsin Greens*), and in the same period the Chippewa tribe sued the State of Wisconsin to ensure spearfishing rights, etc.[84]

Wisconsin experienced its first major and rapid population inflow after the war with the English and Native Americans from 1812-1814. Established as a territory in 1836, Wisconsin gained statehood in 1846, when the majority of Native Americans had already been expelled. The period after the series of revolutions in Europe in 1848-1849 saw the first wave of German immigrants (for example, they already made up 40% of the population of Milwaukee by 1848). Apart from bringing beer and cheese production with them, these newcomers carried liberal ideas whose influence would not be suppressed until World War One. Mathilde Franziska Anneke, a political refugee from Germany, founded the first women's magazine in Milwaukee. The strength of the German influence is reflected in the success of the mutiny caused by the attempt to introduce the English language into German schools in 1889. Marxism was very popular among German workers (for a long period it was known as 'German philosophy' in Wisconsin), and its non-revolutionary version was in particular advocated by Victor Berger and Richard T. Ely.

At the beginning of the 20th century, the Governor (and later Senator) of Wisconsin Robert M. LaFolette advocated a programme of so-called progressivism, which eventually provided a framework for public education, and introduced terms and topics such as 'public opinion', 'public interest', civil activism, and ecology into public discourse. LaFolette, who moved the masses with his speeches that he held while standing on a car and at crossroads, and who married a lawyer-suffragette and advocate of the rights of Black Americans, is remembered for his struggle against corporations, and his associate Charles

---

[83] Patty Loew, *Seventh Generation Earth Ethics: Native Voices of Wisconsin* (Madison: Wisconsin Historical Society Press, 2014), 5.

[84] For a more detailed analysis of these and other Wisconsin influences on Potter's bioethics, see Amir Muzur, Iva Rinčić and Stephen O. Sodeke, 'The real Wisconsin Idea: The seven pillars of Van Rensselaer Potter's bioethics', *Journal of Agricultural and Environmental Ethics* 29, no. 4 (2016): 587-596

McCarthy as the founder of the 'legal library' and professional and educational courses. Wisconsin was also the place where the Republican Party was founded, and in 1853 it became the first federal state which abolished the death penalty. Robert LaFolette's brother, Phil, who later also became governor, was the first in the USA to adopt a law on unemployment benefits and to introduce public works, and in 1935 he obtained 100 million dollars from the federal government for soil conservation, erosion control, hunting and fishing management, and afforestation.

Environmental issues appeared early on. Around 1840, the economy switched from the fur trade to logging (especially pines) in the north of Wisconsin (this is where tourism later started to develop with wealthy people camping out in the countryside in the 1920s) and agriculture in the south. As early as 1878, William W. Daniells, Professor at the University of Wisconsin, was pointing out that the way of cultivating wheat that was being used was destroying the soil (he called it *land skimming*) if one did not invest anything in it. (The German immigrants, however, had brought with them the practice of fertilising, which significantly improved the situation, and they also brought dairy farming, which later surpassed growing crops.) Another professor at the University, William A. Henry (Dean of the College of Agriculture), established in around 1881 that grain stored in silos loses only 10% of its nutritional value, while hay loses up to 50% in the same period. Henry's discovery resulted in a revolution in livestock breeding. This was at a time when Madison (named after the American president), and other towns in Wisconsin, did not have water supply, sewage and garbage collection systems, and cows still freely walked the streets.[85]

The University in Madison was often the epicentre of the Native American struggle for the environment. It is hard to believe that the institution, to which Potter was attached for more than six decades, did not leave a deep mark on his intellectual development. The University of Wisconsin-Madison, according to rankings that are widely used in America, is one of the better higher education institutes in the country. In the *U. S. News & World Report* list of colleges it was ranked 47th in the USA, while in the list of universities it was ranked 27th in the world. Established in 1848, the University today has 20 schools and colleges, more than 40,000 students, and 11 Nobel Prize laureates in its history. It is categorised as a university with 'very high scientific-research activity' (RU/VH; in 2012 it had a research expenditure of $1.1 billion, the third highest in the USA). Several figures made this university world famous: Edward Birge and Chancey Juday studied Lake Mendota and established the foundations for modern limnology; Stephen Babcock came up with the test for determining dairy fat; Harry L. Russell introduced the bovine tuberculin test; Harry

[85] For more on the history of Wisconsin, see Norman K. Risjord, *Wisconsin: The Story of the Badger State* (Madison: Wisconsin Tails & Trials, 1995).

Steenbock (1886-1967) discovered that exposure to UV rays increased the content of vitamin D in milk and other organic matter and could be used in the treatment of rickets (for this, he was twice nominated for the Nobel Prize). Karl Paul Link and his students isolated dicoumarol and proved its anticoagulant effect. It was later used as a poison for rodents and in the drug warfarin (from WARF, *Wisconsin Alumni Research Foundation*). Henry A. Lardy (1917-2010) earned his bachelor's degree (like V. R. Potter) at the South Dakota State College, and later dedicated himself to chemistry and the dairy industry. At Madison University, where he earned his master's and PhD degrees in the 1940s, he was the team leader of the Enzyme Institute and gained fame (in 1958 he became a member of the National Academy of Sciences) as one of the inventors of the adjustable micropipette, and particularly for developing methods for the storage and preservation of semen, which aided artificial insemination in livestock. The University of Wisconsin-Madison is today a large building site. Entirely new towers are being opened with laboratories: the Wisconsin Institutes for Discovery, a public-private institution that includes two interdisciplinary institutes.

The University of Wisconsin was often the source of social turbulence. In 1894, the socialist economist Richard T. Ely (founder of the *Land Economics* magazine, in which Potter also published) provided support to a strike of printing house workers and was accused of 'supporting revolutionary doctrines and violence', but the University investigating commission defended Ely and academic freedom, asserting that the fearless *sifting and winnowing* of social phenomena should even be encouraged.

After a series of demonstrations against the war that the Americans were conducting in Vietnam and Cambodia (and bloody protests across the USA), in August 1970 a bomb exploded that was aimed at destroying the Army Mathematics Research Center at the University of Wisconsin. The explosion killed an innocent post-doctoral physics researcher.

It is therefore no wonder that in an atmosphere characterised by a longing for peace, disarmament and freedom, the American national project to mark *Earth Day*[86] was launched in Madison on 22 April 1970. Exhibitions, public discussions, lectures and films took place across an entire week, and people got together on picnics and 'confessed their sins' towards the environment. Above all, this was due to the initiative of Wisconsin senator Gaylord Nelson, but it also had the active participation of Potter and many other university teachers and students. Journalist Whitney Gould saw this 'environmental mania' as a 'new

[86] As it is no wonder that the city of Madison later embraced the 'Natural Step' philosophy and incorporated it into its sustainable development plans.

religion' – a kind of bio-ethics,[87] thus introducing into daily publications the new term which had appeared at the same time in scientific literature thanks to Potter. It is interesting that Gould's article has the word 'bio-ethics' spelled with a hyphen, which resembles Fritz Jahr's use of the word, and ascribes the thesis that 'fear of the Lord is the beginning of wisdom' to Potter, which, considering Potter's reservations with regard to religion, seems unlikely. (On one occasion, much later, a year before his death, Potter noted, commenting on the United Nations Millennium Declaration that had been adopted by the UN General Assembly in the year 2000: 'Is it so that global bioethics cannot be declared national or international policy only because it mentions *ethics* without mentioning *God*? What do you think of global bioethics as the *codex of nature and a natural God*?'[88] Members of Potter's 'Network' were not exactly delighted with this proposal which, because it mentioned God, 'would make some people whose participation is crucial in global bioethics distance themselves from it'.)

As a direct consequence of *Earth Day* and the general mood that followed, the same year saw the establishment of the *US Environmental Protection Agency*, *Environmental Action*, and the *Natural Resources Defense Council*. In the period from 1971 to 1974, the US adopted a series of acts, including the Marine Mammal Protection Act, the Clean Water Act, the Endangered Species Preservation Act, the National Reserves Management Act, and others. This was also the time when the famous *Blue Marble* image of the Earth was taken from *Apollo 1* and when DDT was banned. Obviously, the 1970s can be regarded as a time when environmentalism was born as an ideology and social movement based partly on Erich Fromm's idea of 'biophilia', which was later popularised by Edward O. Wilson as the 'tendency to seek connections with other forms of life'. (However, Potter did not think particularly highly of Wilson because of his extreme reductionism.)[89] Almost at the same time, environmentalism started taking strong roots in Europe too. For example, the 'G. Gadio' Group for Basic Ecology (*Gruppo 'G. Gadio' per l'Ecologia di base*, named after the street where it had emerged) was established in Milan in May 1971, gathering university

[87] Whitney Gould, 'Bio-ethics creed emerges from 'E-Week' observance as a new type of religion', *Madison Capital Times*, 25 April 1970. (Gould became famous for exposing nitrate pollution in Lake Monona.)

[88] Van Rensselaer Potter, e-mail to the 'Global bioethics network', dated 12 September 2000. DICEB *Fritz Jahr* Archive SuRi – IŠ – VRP 1.

[89] Cf. Michael S. Gregory, 'Science and humanities: Toward a new worldview', in *The Culture of Biomedicine, Studies in Science and Culture*, vol. 1, eds. Heyward Brock and Ann Harward (Newark/London/Toronto: University of Delaware Press / Associated University Press, 1984), 25 (11-33).

teachers, museum professionals and amateurs around environmental ideas and activities.[90]

Potter's public engagement in the 1960s also had other directions. One of the projects which caught V. R. Potter's attention (and active participation) was the *Monona Terrace* project of the *Community and Convention Center* that had been completed by Frank Lloyd Wright back in 1938. The project, which was abandoned during World War Two (some claim it was because of disgust with the eccentric, arrogant and 'amoral' Lloyd Wright), was revived in 1954, and Potter took part in its promotion as an activist of the *Citizens for a Civic Center* movement (one of its prominent supporters was Henry Lardy, while Potter eventually became its president). Despite great controversy in the City Council, Potter was elected to the 12-member committee ('Auditorium') that was to consider the project.[91] However, it all ended in failure, as Mayor Otto Festge lost the elections, and the project, on six levels, was only realised in 1997 (in 2005 alone, the centre earned more than 52 million dollars from conferences and other activities).

It is possible that Potter's connection to F. Lloyd Wright's ideas was even deeper than Monona. Born as Frank Lincoln[92] Wright in 1867 in the small town of Richland Center in Wisconsin to a family of Welsh origin, his early childhood was strongly connected to the natural landscapes of Wisconsin, which he later transformed into his general views of creation and life. After having learned from some of the greatest architects in Chicago such as Louis Sullivan and Dankmar Adler, Lloyd Wright developed his own vision and opened his own office. His ambition of living in harmony with nature is probably best depicted in the 'Prairie Style House' which he promoted (it was later called a 'Usonian House'). From the perspective of the contemporary increase in the importance of nature in the life of modern man,[93] Lloyd Wright's contribution became crucial for the concept of 'Organic Architecture.'[94] Wright used the term 'organic' to explain a philosophy that sees Nature as the ultimate model and follows its main principles – kinship of building to ground, decentralisation, natural character,

---

[90] Cf. Cesare F. Sacchi, 'Il Gruppo 'G. Gadio' per l'Ecologia di base: origini e motivi' ['The G. Gadio group for basic ecology: Origins and motives'], *Studi Trentini di Scienze Naturali – Acta Biologica* 78, no. 1 (2001): 13-17.

[91] Cf. Roger Gribble, 'Auditorium unit of 12 confirmed', *Wisconsin State Journal*, 25 June 1965.

[92] After the divorce of his parents, in 1885 he changed his name from Lincoln to Lloyd.

[93] Cf. Andreas Weber, *Sve osjeća: čovjek, priroda i revolucija prirodnih znanosti* [*Everything Feels: Man, Nature and the Revolution in the Natural Sciences*], translated by Boris Perić (Zagreb: Naklada Ljevak, 2011).

[94] There is no confirmation that he is the author of this expression.

tenuity plus continuity, and the view of the third dimension in depth.[95] In Wright's own words:

nothing can live without entity. Now, organic architecture seeks entity, it seeks that completeness in idea in execution which is absolutely true to method, true to purpose, true to character, and is as much the man who lives in it as he is himself ...[96]

If the architecture is never a feature of a building, but of a building reflecting a culture,[97] then Organic Architecture could serve as a reflection of a culture oriented towards nature, especially in Wisconsin. Frank Lloyd Wright had probably never heard of Jahr's term 'bioethics', but he and Potter could have met as members of the same Unitarian community, the *First Unitarian Society of Madison*.[98] Lloyd Wright also constructed the wooden *Unitarian Meeting House*, where Potter gladly went to admire the architecture (and its openness: part of it was visited by Buddhists, Jews and other communities). The Meeting House, built from 1949 to 1951, was listed as a national historical monument in 2004.[99] The testimony of Richard Burgess, who at Potter's urging, had (unsuccessfully) tried to encourage the people of Madison to accept the Monona Terrace project back in the 1970s, that Potter personally knew Lloyd Wright,[100] is however not particularly reliable. During a lecture in 1966 at the First Unitarian Society of Madison, Potter expressed his interest in the utopians Lewis Mumford (1895-1990), Richard Joseph Neutra (1892-1970) and Frank Lloyd Wright (1867-1959), and concluded his admiration for their work by saying 'what a privilege it would be to know all three of them!'[101] Probably, Potter would have prided himself on knowing at least one of them. On the other hand, it is a known fact that the town sociologist and 'organic humanist' Mumford was friends with Lloyd Wright. Potter had, among other things, even quoted

---

[95] Bruce Brooks Pfeiffer, ed., *The Essential Frank Lloyd Wright: Critical Writings on Architecture* (Princeton: Princeton University Press, 2008), 17-18.

[96] Frank Lloyd Wright, 'Organic architecture', in *Truth Against the World*, ed. Patrick J. Meehan (Washington, D.C.: The Preservation Press & National Trust for Historic Preservation, 1992), 51.

[97] Andrew Ballantyne, *Arhitektura* [*Architecture*], translated by Mirzah Purić (Sarajevo: Šahinpašić, 2004), 32.

[98] F. L. Wright not only designed several public buildings in Madison, but during the last decades of his life he lived and worked on a property that he called Taliesin (Welsh: 'shining brow', the name of a legendary poet) in Spring Green in Iowa County in Wisconsin, just 60 kilometres west of the place where a few years later Van Rensselaer Potter conceived of his bioethics. Taliesin was burned down by a disturbed servant, killing seven people, including Lloyd Wright's lover.

[99] Cf. http://fusmadison.org/landmark

[100] Richard Burgess, oral communication, September 2014.

[101] Van Rensselaer Potter, 'The quality of the environment', manuscript dated 31 July 1966. McArdle Laboratory Archive, V. R. Potter.

Mumford's acknowledgement that his (Mumford's) 'actual life, here or anywhere, pushed to the limits of its ideal possibilities'. He was also fond of Mumford's diagnosis that every society, apart from its existing institutions, also has a reservoir of potential (partly rooted in the past) that it is not aware of, and that biology had proven that integrity and balance are qualities to which every organism strives.[102] Richard Neutra, an architect of Austrian origin, (excerpts from his work 'Survival through design' were read before Potter's lecture) was an appropriate model for Potter. He warned that 'if design, production, and construction cannot be channelled to serve survival, if we fabricate an environment — of which, after all, we seem an inseparable part — but cannot make it an organically possible extension of ourselves, then the end of the race may well appear in sight'.[103] Relying on these architectural observations, Potter conceptualised 'seven points on the quality of the environment': 1) basic needs (food, shelter, clothes, space, privacy, leisure and moral and intellectual education) can be satisfied with a certain amount of effort; 2) one should insist on being free of toxic chemicals, unnecessary trauma (primarily from war and traffic) and illnesses that can be prevented; 3) one should demand a culture that respects healthy ecological principles with a long-term perspective; 4) culture has to prepare us and expect flexible answers from each individual; 5) individual happiness should realistically include oscillations between satisfaction and dissatisfaction with a preserved sense of identity; 6) productivity that includes dedication to other members of society; 7) everyone can contribute to the further development of culture and society through a constant pursuit of beauty and order in a way that does not deny the role of individuality and disorder.[104]

The relationship between Potter's ideas and American pragmatism is a separate issue. Henk ten Have tried to connect W. James and Potter's ideas.[105] However, even though Potter always looked for action and responsibility, and was focused on future and progress – thus agreeing with the cardinal points of pragmatism – he never abandoned the abstract level of care for the community and environment, and even often criticised American pragmatism as a mere short-term advantage. At the end of his life, in early 1998, Potter was also attracted to the ideas of George Soros, most likely because of his analysis of the 'global economy', that is the global capitalist system, and his promotion of the idea of a '(global) open society' as a cure for its flaws.[106] Under Soros's influence, Potter in April-May of 2001 outlined in a letter to his 'Network' of global bioethics

[102] Lewis Mumford, *The Story of Utopias* (New York: Viking Press, 1922/1962).

[103] Richard J. Neutra, *Survival through Design* (New York: Oxford University Press, 1954).

[104] Potter, 'The quality of the environment', 6-7. See also: Van Rensselaer Potter, 'The role of the individual in modern society' in *Changing Concepts of Productive Living*, ed. Robert Dean Boyd (Madison: University of Wisconsin – University Extension, 1967), 37-51.

[105] ten Have, 'Potter's notion of bioethics', 68-71.

[106] Cf. George Soros, 'Toward a global open society', *The Atlantic Monthly*, January 1998, 20-32.

supporters (in which he announced a new initiative that saw bioethics as 'a BETTER bridge to the future' or 'the ONLY bridge to the future'), founded the *Center for Bioethical Sustainability* – CBIS – led by Erin Williams, and started 'Project 2050' (which brought the subject of overpopulation back into the focus of global bioethics).[107] Williams decided to establish a branch of the centre in Virginia (*Virginia CBIS*), Sousa-Lennox was appointed the national representative of the Centre in Panama, and Šegota was offered the opportunity to set up a third CBIS in Rijeka[108] (after Wisconsin and Virginia). The person who replaced Potter as the Head of the CBIS was Calvin DeWitt, who was recommended to Potter by Tom Yuill, Head of the Institute of Environmental Studies (IES).[109] (In his message in August 2001, Potter, apart from DeWitt, also mentioned Garet Lahvish, a post-doctoral student from the McArdle, as his successor.)[110]

Potter agreed with Soros's ideas but criticised the work of the economist John Kenneth Galbraith, *The New Industrial State* (2001), reprimanding his disregard for the environment. Potter's ideas were, as expected, well accepted among pacifists, who called for a global biotechnology that would be motivated by global bioethics and which would replace military technology.[111] Although they have not quoted him explicitly, the ideologists of the recent movement of *degrowth* could also easily find something in Potter's ideas.[112]

---

[107] DICEB *Fritz Jahr* Archive SuRi – IŠ – VRP 1.

[108] Van Rensselaer Potter, e-mail to Ivan Šegota and Erin Williams, dated 5 July 2001. DICEB *Fritz Jahr* Archive SuRi – IŠ – VRP 1.

[109] Van Rensselaer Potter, e-mail Ivan Šegota, dated 19 June 2001. DICEB *Fritz Jahr* Archive SuRi – IŠ – VRP 1.

[110] Van Rensselaer Potter, e-mail to the 'Global bioethics network' and John Kenneth Galbraith, dated 27 August 2001. DICEB *Fritz Jahr* Archive SuRi – IŠ – VRP 1.

[111] Cf. Van Rensselaer Potter, 'Professor: Bioethics institutes vital today', *Wisconsin State Journal*, 1 December 1991.

[112] Cf. Giacomo D'Alisa, Federico Demaria and Giorgos Kallis, eds. *Degrowth: A Vocabulary for a New Era*. New York/London: Routledge, 2015.

SILENCED SPRING: DID WASHINGTON AND NEW YORK TAKE OVER BIOETHICS TO SAVE IT OR TO RUIN IT?

In order to better understand the history of bioethics after 1970, one should be aware of different motives behind the conflicts over the authorship of the term 'bioethics' and the concept of the new discipline. Three of these are probably more important: personal vanity, differences between European and American value systems, and the struggle for financial resources. As it is commonly known, André Hellegers (1926-1979), the Dutch obstetrician and foetal physiologist, founded the *Joseph and Rose Fitzgerald Kennedy Institute of Ethics* at Georgetown University in Washington in 1971 together with Eunice and Sargent Shriver. The Institute is located in a building called Healy Hall,[1] which was built in 1877 in the Flemish Neo-romantic style.

Eunice Shriver (1921-2009) was born into the fifth generation of Irish Kennedys in America. Her parents, after whom the Institute in Washington was eventually named, were Joseph Sr. (1888-1969), American ambassador in London during World War Two, and Rose (1890-1995). Her brothers were Joseph (Joe Jr.) (1915-1944; died in World War Two), John (1917-1963; US President from 1961 to 1963), Robert (1925-1968; Attorney General and presidential candidate who, like John, was later assassinated), and Edward (Ted) (1932-2009; Senator). Apart from her four famous brothers, Eunice also had four sisters: Rose Marie (1918-2005; who, suffering from depression, underwent a lobotomy;[2] in order to avoid the term 'mentally ill', the family used the term 'mentally retarded', and even directed the funds of their own foundation towards treating the mentally disabled),[3] Kathleen Agnes (1920-1948), Patricia Helen (1924-2006) and Jean Ann (born in 1928, and the only one still alive). In 1953, Eunice married Robert Sargent Shriver Jr. (1915-2011) in New York. She had five children with him (including their daughter Maria Owings, who later married Arnold Schwarzenegger – bodybuilder, actor and Governor of California). Sargent (Sarge) Shriver, a lawyer and Yale graduate, was known as an active advocate of US neutrality in World War Two, and then as a decorated long-serving volunteer in the US Navy in the Pacific. After the war, he was head of the American Peace Corps for a while and US ambassador in Paris. He even ran unsuccessfully for President of the USA in 1972.[4]

---

[1] Jesuit Patrick Healy was rector at Georgetown University from 1873 to 1882.

[2] She died in the *St Coletta* institution for the mentally disabled in Jefferson, Wisconsin.

[3] Cf. Jon Henley, 'The forgotten Kennedy', *The Guardian*, 13 August 2009 (http://www.theguardian.com/world/2009/aug/13/eunice-kennedy-shriver-rosemary-kennedy)

[4] Cf. Scott Stossel, *Sarge: The Life and Times of Sargent Shriver* (Washington: Smithsonian Books, 2004).

Eunice Kennedy came from a family of practising Catholics, as did Sargent Shriver, who attended Mass each day and carried a worn-out rosary everywhere. Both opponents of abortion and interested in the study of 'mental disabilities', they invested 1.35 million dollars (from the foundation named after Eunice's late brother Joseph Jr.) into founding an institution that was initially called the Institute for the Study of Human Reproduction and Bioethics, but the word 'bioethics' eventually remained only in the name of one centre within the Institute of Ethics, which was led by LeRoy Walters.[5] Among the first to join Hellegers' Institute were Tom Beauchamp and Robert Veatch, and later Edmund Pellegrino, Hans-Martin Sass and others. Over time, the Institute received visits from a series of bioethicists from all over the world – from Ivan Šegota, Valentin Pozaić, Tonči Matulić, Iva Rinčić and Amir Muzur from Croatia to – just as an item of curiosity – the German bioethicist Claire Margarete Lademacher (born in 1985), who later became Princess of Luxembourg.

From the very beginning, the Institute, and its role and ambitions were subject to controversy due to the essentially different concepts of its co-founders and directors. The Institute defined bioethics in a way that was significantly narrower than Potter's concept. In Georgetown, it was required that bioethics deal with 'concrete medical dilemmas' covering three groups of topics: the rights and duties of patients and health workers, the rights and duties of scientists-researchers and subjects (i.e. experimental animals), and drawing up public policy guidelines for clinical work and biomedical research. Today, there are calls to expand the concept and practice of Georgetown bioethics. Potter's namesake, a clinical ethicist from Kansas City in Missouri, Robert Lyman Potter, advocates 'the evolution of bioethics from clinical ethics to organisational ethics of healthcare', because this would, allegedly, involve a broader sociological context, and thus 'a broad ecological version of bioethics'.[6] On the other hand, the Georgetown concept does not think that bioethics needs expanding at all. On the contrary, Tom Beauchamp predicts that the part of bioethics that deals with moral theory will soon disappear, since there is no benefit from it.[7]

The pursuit of originality (which is more profitable in America than anywhere else) led to disagreement in the interpretation of the origin of the term 'bioethics'. Potter told Reich that he had come across the word 'bioethics'

---

[5] Cf. Project on Bioethics in American Society – Interview with LeRoy Walters by Judith P. Swazey, 2000. http://hdl.handle.net/10822/557055

[6] Robert Lyman Potter, 'From clinical ethics to organizational ethics: The second stage of the evolution of bioethics', *Bioethics Forum* (1996): 3-12.

[7] Tom L. Beauchamp, 'Does ethical theory have a future in bioethics?', *Journal of Law, Medicine, and Ethics* 32 (2004): 210 (209-217); cf. H. Tristram Engelhardt, Jr., 'Bioethics after four decades: Looking to the future', speech held upon accepting the Portuguese Bioethics Association Award, 22 May 2012.

suddenly while walking (P. Whitehouse mentioned a bike later on) home from work (the *Eureka! experience*), while Sargent Shriver claimed that inventing the word was *as easy as falling off a log* to him. Shriver's wife Eunice went even further and later on sent Reich an entire story which she, allegedly, remembered well about how her husband Sargent sat one night on the couch, and suddenly, for no particular reason, proposed the name 'bioethics' to Hellegers,[8] and Robert E. Cook, Scientific Advisor to the Joseph P. Kennedy Jr. Foundation, denied his acquaintance with Potter in order to attribute the invention of 'bioethics' to Shriver. Despite these attempts that must have driven Potter mad, Reich, in his two 1990s studies, actually quite clearly argues that Potter 'invented' bioethics and that the founders of the Kennedy Institute appropriated it later on. Nevertheless, Reich's conclusion was careful and considerate, losing its sharpness in the *bilocated birth* thesis, which would mean that both Potter and Hellegers/Shriver arrived at the idea of calling the new discipline by the same name at the same time. Reich even said that Hellegers might have heard Potter's expression and mentioned it to Shriver in an unrelated conversation, so that Shriver later indeed believed that he had coined the term which, actually, had emerged from his subconscious. There is also some self-criticism in Reich's 'Solomonic' explanation, since he admits that he also neglected Potter's role in his early publications, like other American authors. However, Reich remarkably notices that such ignorance of Potter does not apply to literature outside the USA. In addition, the philosopher Daniel Callahan, founder of the New York Hastings Center and one of the first ever bioethicists, and a person that can be regarded impartial with regard to this question, has recently clearly admitted that 'the expression 'bioethics' was first used by the biologist Van Rensselaer Potter.'[9] However, Callahan was not always of this opinion. As an invited lecturer at the 'Interdisciplinary Workshop on the Interrelationships between Science and Technology, and Ethics and Values' (held in April 1975, in Reston, Virginia), Callahan claimed, in front of Potter, that some of his (Callahan's) colleagues and he (i.e. Callahan) had invented bioethics a few years before.[10] When invited to briefly state exactly how bioethics had got its name, in a 1993 issue of the Hastings Center journal Reich claimed more courageously that Potter had invented the word, and Hellegers was the first to use it in the name of an institution (Reich did not even mention Shriver here).[11]

---

[8] Just how important publicity was to the Shrivers can be seen from their aggressive campaign when sponsoring research into mental disabilities at the University of Wisconsin right at the time when Sargent Shriver's political ambitions were greatest. Cf. Doris, 'Land-Grant Ideology', 276.

[9] Cf. Daniel Callahan, 'Bioethics', in *Applied Ethics: Critical Concepts in Philosophy*, eds. Ruth Chedwick and Doris Schroeder (London: Routledge, 2002), 7 (3-19).

[10] Cf. Doris, 'Land-Grant Ideology', 328-329.

[11] Warren T. Reich, 'How bioethics got its name', *The Hastings Center Report* 23, supl. 6 (1993): S6-S7.

The fact remains that in a report about the establishment of the Kennedy Institute, dated at the end of 1970, there is no mention of ethics, let alone bioethics. And while ethics began to emerge in materials connected to the foundation of the Institute in March 1971 (the Institute was formally inaugurated at a press conference on 1 October 1971, which included addresses by Eunice and Sargent Shriver, A. Hellegers, Rector Robert Henle and Edward Kennedy),[12] bioethics was first mentioned only at the end of June. It was around that time – between March and June of 1971 – that 'bioethics' found its way into the media in the USA, primarily thanks to the central theme of the April issue of the widely read *Time* magazine (a special section was entitled 'Man into superman: The promise and peril of the new genetics'.[13] It was featured on the front page, while the text itself mentioned Potter and his, at the time recently published, first book about bioethics). It should also be mentioned that Eunice Shriver knew of the *Time* April issue and that Hellegers used to read *Perspectives in Biology and Medicine* (which was sometimes labelled a hermeticist or elitist journal) in which Potter had used the term 'bioethics' as early as 1970.[14] At some point later in time, Potter even called bioethics an 'orphan' not accepted by either environmental or medical ethics due to Hellegers' ignorance.[15] Regarding the establishment of the Institute, he said that philosophers got hold of the word without paying attention to its source and premises and started establishing institutes for bioethics.[16]

The term quickly spread in the media, partly under the influence of Potter's publications, but even more due to the campaign from Georgetown. When addressing the American Association for Cancer Research, Potter noticed as early as 1975 that 'Georgetown's understanding of bioethics is restricted to ethical questions around the 'right to live', about artificial prolongation of life without meaning, death with dignity, and human experimentation – ethical decisions regarding the wisdom of when to do and when to leave be' and pointed out that his 'own view of bioethics calls for a much broader vision. It calls for a wider and more purposeful understanding of biological evolution and cultural

---

[12] Cf. Warren Thomas Reich, 'Revisiting the launching of the Kennedy Institute: Re-visioning the origins of bioethics', *Kennedy Institute of Ethics Journal* 6, no. 4 (1996): 323-327.

[13] 'Man into superman: The promise and peril of the new genetics', *Time*, 19 April 1971, 33-52.

[14] Warren Thomas Reich, 'The word 'bioethics': Its birth and the legacies of those who shaped it', *Kennedy Institute of Ethics Journal* 4, no. 4 (1994): 326-327 (319-335); cf. also Warren Thomas Reich, 'The word 'bioethics': The struggle over its earliest meanings', *Kennedy Institute of Ethics Journal* 5, no. 1 (1995): 19-34.

[15] Van Rensselaer Potter, 'Global Bioethics: Origin and development', in *Handbook for Environmental Risk Decision Making: Values, Perceptions, and Ethics*, ed. C. Richard Cothern (Boca Raton: CRC Lewis Publishers, 1996), 359-373.

[16] Cf. Potter, 'Professor: Bioethics institutes vital today'.

evolution'.[17] (The idea of the necessity of a 'delicate balance between biological and cultural evolution' would be taken over from Potter and further developed by James Trosko.)[18] However, four years later, Potter, in a newspaper response to the Three Mile Island accident, seemed somewhat defeated. He wrote of a wrong interpretation and understanding of bioethics, about the fact that 'the word may have lost its usefulness' and that there were already 'professors of bioethics' who advocate the idea that bioethics is that which suits the modern needs of people.[19]

Even within the University of Wisconsin in Madison, a group emerged as early as 1973 that began developing a multidisciplinary programme of medical ethics which was eventually transformed into 'bioethics'. This Madison version of the Kennedy Institute has been led by the paediatrician Norman Frost, who himself does not seem to find many common points in his and Potter's work.[20]

Someone might say that Hellegers saved Potter's idea from oblivion by founding the Institute, that is, by institutionalising it. Yet Hellegers' relationship towards Potter was more than mysterious. Potter claimed Hellegers had never contacted him.[21] Warren Thomas Reich, devoted student and friend of Hellegers, compared his charm to Fred Astaire's. According to Reich, Hellegers, son of a banker, an Edinburgh and Paris student, and later a Yale and Johns Hopkins scholar (he arrived in the United States in 1953, and in 1958 studied foetal breathing at high altitudes in Peru), introduced interdisciplinary and ecumenical practices, and won the Kennedy's financial support (Georgetown) even though Dan Callahan had applied for it before him. Hellegers wanted the Institute to be incorporated into the clinic, but the idea was never realised. In the 1960s, he participated in the work of the Pontifical Commission for the Study of Population, Family and Birth, and – even though he was a convinced Catholic – he changed his opinion to the extent that he commented on the work of the Commission by saying –'the discussions have convinced me more of the danger of inflexible attitudes than of the evil of contraception'. He died at the age 52, embittered with the administration of the Institute, which had wanted him to receive his salary solely from projects.[22] Reich has always claimed that his European 'broad'

---

[17] Potter, 'Humility with responsibility', 2300.

[18] Cf. James E. Trosko, 'Scientific views of human nature: Implications for the ethics of technological intervention', in *The Culture of Biomedicine, Studies in Science and Culture*, vol. 1, eds. Heyward Brock and Ann Harward (Newark/London/Toronto: University of Delaware Press / Associated University Press, 1984), 85 (70-97).

[19] Van Rensselaer Potter, 'Bioethics looks at survival with a long view', *Madison Capital Times*, 9 April 1979.

[20] Norman Frost, e-mail, 1 October 2014.

[21] Potter, *Bioetika: most prema budućnosti* [*Bioethics: Bridge to the Future*], 257.

[22] Warren Thomas Reich, 'The 'wider view': André Hellegers' passionate, integrating intellect and the creation of bioethics', *Kennedy Institute of Ethics Journal* 9, no. 1 (1999): 25-51.

horizons differentiated Hellegers significantly from his American colleagues at Georgetown.[23]

The second influential institution in America (actually the first in terms of age) that dealt with bioethics – the Hastings Center in New York – treated Potter and his ideas in a very similar way. The centre was founded in 1969 in Hastings-on-Hudson (in the northern suburbs of New York), the little town it was named after, although it has relocated twice since. Now it operates in the small town of Garrison, 90 miles north of New York City, upstream on the River Hudson. The Center was founded by the philosopher Daniel Callahan (born in 1930, and educated in part at Georgetown University) and the psychiatrist-psychoanalyst Willard Gaylin. Its ideas were somewhat different from Georgetown's. Among other things, the Center was autonomous from the beginning, i.e. not dependent on the university (which resulted in the fact that at first it had to be financially supported by Callahan's mother, as well as the Rockefellers, and that it was first located in Callahan's apartment).[24] Of course, in his 'Preliminary Sketch' (1968-1969) about the establishment of the Center, Callahan does not mention bioethics or 'the biological revolution', but in 1970 he directed his attention and action programme more clearly towards the ethical aspects of the 'biological revolution' (by which he meant biomedical research and its results), the 'population explosion' and the 'environmental crisis' – thus moving closer to Potter than the Georgetown group. As the *Kennedy Institute of Ethics* publishes its *Kennedy Institute of Ethics Journal*, so the Hastings Center publishes the *Hastings Center Report* and *IRB: A Review of Human Subjects Research*.

Considering that 'he invented bioethics with his colleagues', as he himself claimed in 1975, Callahan has always been fairly imprecise in using this term, constantly interchanging it with 'biomedical ethics', and he has also confessed a few times that the name bioethics had no real appeal to him, since he first of all wanted to be (considered) a moral philosopher,[25] and that he used this name reluctantly.[26] (In the Anglophone world, Callahan's attitude is of course not a rarity. When he was asked at a conference in Belgrade to explain the difference between 'medical ethics' and 'bioethics', Don Marquis answered that he did not know. The *Cambridge Quarterly of Healthcare Ethics* journal even has the subtitle 'A quarterly journal devoted to engaging a world community of bioethicists', and the first sentence of the foreword to the seventh edition of the

---

[23] Warren Thomas Reich, oral communication, September 2014.

[24] M. L. Tina Stevens, *Bioethics in America: Origins and Cultural Politics* (Baltimore/London: Johns Hopkins University Press, 2000), 50-51.

[25] Daniel Callahan, *In Search of the Good: A Life in Bioethics* (Cambridge: MIT Press, 2012), 53.

[26] Cf. Reich, 'How bioethics got its name'.

famous 'Principles of Biomedical Ethics' by Tom Beauchamp and James Childress starts with: 'Biomedical ethics, or bioethics… ')[27]

In his review of the series of a dozen publications up to 1981 that originated from the Hastings Center, Potter objected that the Center completely disregarded the work of Aldo Leopold, and that with its choice of staff (i.e. *non-biologists*, as all members had socio-humanities backgrounds) it was not capable of recognising or assessing the necessity of the environmental aspect of bioethics.[28] It is interesting to note that today the Hastings Center is intensively turning towards environmental ethics, but – as if it even needs to be mentioned – without referring to Potter (and even less to Jahr). In his most recent book *Humans in Nature: The World as We Find it and the World as We Create it*, Gregory Kaebnick, editor of *The Hastings Center Report*, discusses the boundaries between the natural and the artificial. Although he sympathises with the attitude of the 'Friends of Nature' movement, which regards DNA manipulation as crossing the border of the allowable and reasonable, he still advocates a sort of 'middle way' by revealing a certain liberalism when it comes to human interventions in nature.[29]

V. R. Potter's last message to the network of his followers reveals a frustration with the insufficient personal acknowledgement that he had received in the USA.[30] For example, in an article from 1996, Potter asks directly: 'Why was I so successful when I wrote articles and reports on cancer research, and so unrecognized in the United States when I started writing about ethical issues?'[31] It is possible that such a mood, along with an overall disappointment with the narrowing of bioethics to a 'new medical ethics', resulted in Potter's concept of 'global bioethics' in the late 1980s. This was probably driven by his wish to be original once again but also to move bioethics from the USA to other cultures and continents.[32] Potter said that he was able to write the book *Global Bioethics: Building on the Leopold Legacy* (published in 1988) only after he had withdrawn from research and teaching, but the general impression, however, is that the book was created primarily under the influence of certain personal events (as he himself says, 'by 1988 it had become clear that the word bioethics

---

[27] Tom L. Beauchamp and James F. Childress, *Principles of Biomedical Ethics*, 7th edition (New York/Oxford: Oxford University Press, 2013), vii.

[28] Van Rensselaer Potter, 'Bioethics: State-of-the-art books', *BioScience* 31, no. 2 (1981): 172.

[29] Gregory E. Kaebnick, *Humans in Nature: The World as We Find it and the World as We Create it* (Oxford/New York: Oxford University Press, 2014).

[30] Cf. Van Rensselaer Potter, 'The intellectual *last will* of the first global bioethicist', in *Fritz Jahr and the Foundations of Global Bioethics: The Future of Integrative Bioethics*, eds. Amir Muzur and Hans-Martin Sass (Münster: Lit, 2012): 155 (149-157).

[31] Van Rensselaer Potter, 'What does bioethics mean?', *The Ag Bioethics Forum* 8, no. 1 (1996) (http://www.bioethics.iastate.edu/forum/jun.96pg2.html).

[32] Potter, *Global Bioethics*.

had completely slipped out of my hands').[33] The frustrations that changed Potter's attitudes also changed the development of bioethics in general, which once again demonstrates the importance of tracing the life path of a person if one wants to completely understand ideas.[34]

It is interesting that Potter considered writing the book *Understanding Global Bioethics* for the publisher *Johns Hopkins University Press*. In a letter of January 1996, he asked W. Reich to let him have his two articles on the origin of bioethics (obviously this refers to Reich's articles that were published in 1994 and 1995 respectively in the *Kennedy Institute of Ethics Journal*), which Potter would then publish as the opening chapters of his new book.[35] In the mid-1970s, Potter also reportedly worked with J. Trosko on the book *Biology for Humanity*.

Things however finally changed in the last decade of Potter's life thanks to Brunetto Chiarelli and his very dynamic support of global bioethics (including the launch of the *Global Bioethics* journal in English, which not only brought Potter his long-awaited acknowledgement but also opened new opportunities for him). Potter travelled to a conference in Trento, and then, at the Third International Bioethics Seminar in 1993, the Japanese philosopher Masahiro Morioka (born in 1958) promoted Potter and his ideas in the best possible way by criticising 'today's principle-based, male-centered, medicine-oriented, American bioethics' and advocated a bioethics that would be an 'international, cross-cultural, more feminist, more environmentally-oriented study of life, science and society'.[36] In 1998, another Japanese bioethicist, Hyakudai Sakamoto,[37] invited Potter to the Fourth Congress of the International Association of Bioethics. Potter did not travel to Tokyo but sent his (first) video-tape with a recorded speech – something that he continued doing until the end of his life. Sakamoto made Potter's tape into a transcript and distributed it among the participants. In 9 pages, it describes the different development phases of bioethics – 'bridge', 'global', and 'deep', where 'bridge' is first explained as a 'bridge to the future', and then as a 'bridge among disciplines'.[38] Potter continued to receive invitations to conferences in the following years – to Bogota (1998), Mexico City (to the Third Latin American and Caribbean Congress in November 1999; Potter was invited by Manuel Velasco Suárez, 1914-2001,

---

[33] Potter, 'What does bioethics mean?'.

[34] Part of this text was taken from Rinčić and Muzur, *Fritz Jahr i rađanje europske bioetike* [*Fritz Jahr and the Emergence of European Bioethics*], 79-85.

[35] McArdle Laboratory archive, V. R. Potter, box no. 4.

[36] Cf. Doris, 'Land-Grant Ideology', 378.

[37] Cf. Hyakudai Sakamoto, 'Towards a new 'Global Bioethics'', *Bioethics* 13, no. 3-4 (1999): 191-197.

[38] *Script for a Videotape for Tokyo, November 1998 (copyright©1998 Van Rensselaer Potter): Permission to copy and distribute granted to Prof. Hyakudai Sakamoto*. DICEB *Fritz Jahr* Archive SuRi – IŠ – VRP 1.

neurologist, neurosurgeon, President of the National Committee for Bioethics and Governor of Chiapas 1970-1976), to Panama (in May 2000; the invitation came from the odontologist Eduardo Enrique Sousa-Lennox Mendoza), to Gijón in Spain (in June 2000, at the invitation of Marcel Palacios, born in 1934, and deputy in the Spanish Parliament 1982-1996; a result of the First World Conference on Bioethics was the adoption of the Bioethics Declaration of Gijón, and Potter's address – according to the transcript of the video tape – focused primarily on Lester Brown),[39] then to Caracas (in February 2001), and finally to the island of Cres in Croatia,[40] where Potter was invited in September 2001 by another member of his 'Global Bioethics Network', the promoter of bioethics from Rijeka, Ivan Šegota (1938-2011). In his last address via video tape, Potter thanked both Ivan Šegota and Ante Čović. As is well known, Čović established the 'Lošinj Days of Bioethics', the largest annual meeting of bioethicists in South-East Europe.

At the end of March 2001, only six months before his death, Potter brought together the *Global Bioethics Core Group*. Apart from Potter as its president, the group included individuals who held strong beliefs about what constituted global bioethics and who supported its concept in their own way, without the obligation of supporting the views developed by the original proponent: Brunetto Chiarelli, Hyakudai Sakamoto, Peter Whitehouse, and Hans Schweinsberg (President of the Canadian International Institute of the Sciences, Humanities and Global Bioethics in Toronto), Michael Fox (Washington), Erin D. Williams (George Mason University in Virginia) and Heinz Herrmann (Connecticut University emeritus). Apart from the 'Core', a further eleven supporters of global bioethics in Europe and Latin America were listed (among them Ivan Šegota), as well as a list of some fifteen books, documents, and institutions whose contributions to global bioethics were particularly valued. The UN Universal Declaration of Human Rights, Aldo Leopold, the Lester Brown Worldwatch Institute, *The Turning Point* Project (founded in 1999 and dedicated to publishing articles about the ecological crisis), the International Center for Technology Assessment (CTA), the 'Natural Step' movement (TNS), the Paul Hawke's Natural Resources Institute, the Union of Concerned Scientists (UCS), Michael W. Fox's book *Bringing Life to Ethics: Global Bioethics for a Humane Society* (which was still in print in 2001), and five other books on evolutionary psychology, reform of the economy, globalisation and holistic management. The list also included 43 of Potter's publications under the title 'The Development of the ethical concepts

[39] Van Rensselaer Potter, 'Bioethical issues for the 21st century', script for a videotape presentation at the opening ceremony of the World Conference on Bioethics, Gijón, Spain, June 20-24, 2000. DICEB *Fritz Jahr* Archive SuRi – IŠ – VRP 1.

[40] Despite the announcement, the conference actually took place on the island of Lošinj.

of Van Rensselaer Potter after 1962, while he continued publishing papers on cancer research until 1988.'[41]

Michael Fox, a London veterinary surgeon who studied medicine and ethology and who taught psychology, was a tireless animal rights campaigner,[42] a prodigious writer and a fighter against the 'spiritual corruption' which by abusing biotechnology had led to 'genetic imperialism'.[43] He embraced Potter's global bioethics as *ethics for life and for living* and 'biosophy' (that is, the wisdom derived from the scientific, especially biological and ecological, and empathic perception of life).[44] Potter received Fox's book *Global Bioethics for a Humane Society* in January 2001, with the author's dedication. On the first page of the introduction, Fox, referring to his own holistic concept of bioethics that seeks 'to integrate various disciplines and spheres of concern', acknowledges Potter for 'identifying the integrative, interdisciplinary ('bridge') functions of bioethics'.[45]

In his last letter to the members of his 'Network', Potter apologised for not having included others in the 'Core', especially Ivan Šegota and Marcel Palacios (who had invited him in the meantime to attend conferences in Cres/Lošinj and Gijón), concluding that the 'Core' was actually just a source group that had grown. (In an e-mail to Šegota in June 2000, Potter even suggested that Šegota, Arturo Filipowicz - a young priest from Warsaw who was preparing a bioethics master's thesis at that time, and Thomas Potthast from Berlin, should become the 'New Core' of global bioethics.)[46] In a continuation of his last letter, Potter complained that in the period from 1970 to 1990 there was no one to recognise and follow him and that by 1988 'only one person in the entire world' had noticed the book on global bioethics: Brunetto Chiarelli. The network was subsequently joined by Peter Whitehouse (1996-7), Hans Schweinsberg, Erin Williams, and others. Finally, Potter recommended to the members of his 'Network' to support Calvin DeWitt and work together with Thomas Potthast, who was writing a history of bioethics, and listed the 38 names and e-mail addresses of the 'Network' members. That the 'Network' changed in size can be seen from an e-mail of June 1999 in which Potter sent a circular letter to only 23 addresses (including Peter Singer, Warren Reich, Darryl Macer and some others that cannot be found on the list of recipients of Potters 'last will'). In another

[41] DICEB *Fritz Jahr* Archive SuRi – IŠ – VRP 1.
[42] Cf. Michael W. Fox, *Inhumane Society: The American Way of Exploiting Animals* (New York: St. Martin's Press, 1990).
[43] Cf. Michael W. Fox, *Beyond Evolution: The Genetically Altered Future of Plants, Animals, the Earth... and Humans* (New York: The Lyons Press, 1999).
[44] Michael W. Fox, *Bringing Life to Ethics: Global Bioethics for a Humane Society* (Albany: State University of New York Press, 2001), 27-29.
[45] Ibid., 1.
[46] Van Rensselaer Potter, e-mail to Ivan Šegota, dated 14 June 2000. DICEB *Fritz Jahr* Archive SuRi – IŠ – VRP 1.

address in June 1999, Potter did not give up the name 'International Society for Global Bioethics', although his attention was drawn to the fact that, given the (erroneous) understanding of bioethics, this could be interpreted as a 'Global Ethics of Healthcare'. However, after a 'eureka-effect' which he had had the weekend before, he said 'the word [bioethics] needs to speak for itself'. It appears that Warren Reich tried to persuade Potter to give up the new name (in Potters words, 'when Warren Reich speaks, we all have to listen'), suggesting the establishment of a section within the existing International Association for Bioethics (IAB), which however seemed unacceptable to Potter. Potter, in front of his 'Network' forum, embarked on an e-mail dispute with Reich, accusing him of insisting on the ambiguity of the term 'global'. It is true, however, that while some authors advocated the harmonisation and integration of bioethical ideas to achieve the idea of global bioethics,[47] others used more empirical methods (by analysing online content) to try to prove that global bioethics did not exist.[48]

In fact, the American bioethics which was appropriated by the Kennedy Institute of Ethics and turned in the direction of the 'four principles mantra' is today being criticised[49] and attacked as narrow, uniculturocentric and 'boring'[50] to such an extent that a return to Potter's ideas (not to mention the refreshment of Jahr) has become almost necessary. (Of course, 'American bioethics' is often the only bioethics that people in the USA know about, being considered also problematic because it 'slows down' the development of science. It is therefore no wonder that Steven Pinker recently claimed that the only task of contemporary bioethics is 'to get out of the way'.) Despite everything, Potter was right to say that 'the concept of global bioethics, which will continue to live under whatever name, no longer needs him',[51] although he recognised that the 'viable survival' in the vision of global bioethics is actually utopian.[52] Admittedly, one could have said that in Margaret Mead's ambitious optimism or in John Platt's dreamlike style

[47] Hans-Martin Sass and Zhai Xiaomei, 'Global Bioethics: Eastern or Western principles?', *Asian Bioethics Review* 3, no. 1 (2011): 1-2.

[48] Søren Holm and Bryn Williams-Jones, 'Global bioethics – Myth or reality?', *BMC Medical Ethics* 7, no. 10 (2006): 1-10.

[49] Cf., for example, the valid criticism in: Roberto Dell'Oro, 'Oltre la censura del senso: riflessioni sul futuro della bioetica' ['Beyond the censorship of meaning: Reflections on the future of bioethics'], *Medicina e morale* 63, no. 2 (2014): 233-246.

[50] Cf. Albert R. Jonsen, 'Why has bioethics become so boring?' *Journal of Medical Philosophy* 25, no. 6 (2000): 689-699; Dianne N. Irving, 'The bioethics mess', *Crisis Magazine* 19, no. 5 (2001); Gary S. Belkin, 'Moving beyond bioethics: History and the search for medical humanism', *Perspectives in Biology and Medicine* 47, no. 3 (2004): 374, etc.

[51] Potter, 'What does bioethics mean?'.

[52] Van Rensselaer Potter, 'Moving the culture toward more vivid utopias with survival as the goal', *Global Bioethics* 14, no. 4 (2001): 19-30.

claiming that 'the world has now become too dangerous for anything less than Utopia'.[53]

[53] Platt, *The Step to Man*.

FATHERS AND FEATHERS: WHAT V. R. POTTER GAINED, AND WHAT HE LOST AFTER THE DISCOVERY OF FRITZ JAHR'S WORK

When writing about the origin of the word 'bioethics', W. Reich came up with the *bilocated birth* hypothesis. Had he known about Fritz Jahr's bioethics, he could have named it *bitemporal*.

The discovery of Fritz Jahr's work, which as we know occurred in 1997 thanks to a report by Rolf Löther, and then spread around the world, particularly in South America, Europe[1] and Asia,[2] had the least effect in the USA. Even Margaret Doris, in her otherwise very meticulous approach to (American) sources, mentioning Fritz Jahr in the 6th footnote of her comprehensive dissertation, reveals that she knows of (only) one book about Jahr in English,[3] and two of Sass's articles about him. Doris's comment that 'While I am not unsympathetic to the enthusiasm Jahr's bio-ethik has inspired, I rather liken it to Leonardo's helicopter: elegant on paper, but never built, never flown', reveals a very frequent reaction of those who write about the history of bioethics. Almost as if they feel sorry that someone new and relevant has appeared, these authors mention Jahr only in a footnote or, in the best case, dedicate a paragraph to him, trying to prevent this inconvenient fact from disturbing the completed and therefore perfect flow of their thoughts and text. Just as Daniel Kehlmann in his essay 'Wo ist Carlos Montúfar?' claims that writers start to adopt the characters of their stories as if they were entirely the fruit of their imagination, so Doris (and many others) adopt Potter and try to protect him from 'intruders' in a rather abstract way. In her pedantry, Margaret Doris wants to show that she knows about Jahr, but at the same time she strives at any cost to diminish the significance of the fact that she actually does not know him. She even explicitly emphasises that 'Deploying Jahr's bioethics now, either as an academic or practical exercise, does not in any way suggest it inspired or influenced the development of bioethics prior to Lother's (re)discovery of his work'.[4]

---

[1] Among the first in Europe, after authors in Germany and Croatia, to spread the news about Jahr was the editor of the *Medicina e morale* journal from Rome, Alberto Spagnolo. Cf. Antonio G. Spagnolo,'L'imperativo bioetico' ['The bioethical imperative'], *Medicina e morale* 1 (2010): 9-14.

[2] For more information on this, see Rinčić and Muzur, *Fritz Jahr i rađanje europske bioetike* [*Fritz Jahr and the Emergence of European Bioethics*], 127-141.

[3] Amir Muzur and Hans-Martin Sass, eds., *Fritz Jahr and the Foundations of Global Bioethics: The Future of Integrative Bioethics* (Münster: Lit, 2012).

[4] Cf. Doris,'Land-Grant Ideology', 2-3.

Other experiences with Jahr in the USA have been similar. The *American Journal of Bioethics* refused to publish an article by the authors of this book about Jahr by claiming that 'this journal has already published papers on the subject of deepening Potter's bioethics and is ready to do so in the future'. Hans-Martin Sass, a tireless promoter of Jahr and his work around the world, has tried to acquaint some of his colleagues from the Kennedy Institute of Ethics with Jahr. The interest that they showed was anything but encouraging. In any case, trying to propagate Fritz Jahr in the USA is a difficult task. Just as A. Leopold spoke of the '*biotic arrogance of Homo Americanus*', one could also speak about the '*bioethical arrogance of Homo Americanus*'.

Apart from their fates, F. Jahr and V. R. Potter also share certain biographical similarities. For example, they both had to take care of their ill wives, and they also shared a fascination (as did Aldo Leopold) with Charles Darwin and evolution. However, the differences in their lives and ideas are much greater. Potter was recognised, at least as an oncologist, in his lifetime, while Jahr was not. There are also some differences in their two (wider) ethics. Although they were both occupied with sexual instinct, Potter saw in it today a useless cause of overpopulation (but also of violence in the family, pornography, and gender inequality), while Jahr, expectedly, moralised about the 'unacceptability' of masturbation and homosexuality.[5] Both Potter and Jahr sensed the importance of education. Potter defined the 'ten most important themes' and Jahr 'ten principles' of teaching.[6]

Fritz Jahr's and Van Rensselaer Potter's bioethics also have intriguing similarities and differences. One difference is undoubtedly Jahr's unconditional trust in science (Jahr's bioethics was coined as a consequence of the progress of physiology and 'biopsychics') while Potter feared the immaturity of science, its unpreparedness to cope with its own achievements, and its divergence from ethical values. By directing science towards the humanities and vice versa, Potter, however, gladly emphasised that medicine, as applied biology, should not learn only from molecular biology and genetics but also from evolutionism and ecology. Jahr saw undisputed guidelines in religion. Potter, however, advocated that religion should adopt scientific discoveries and integrate its views with those of science. Potter was, expectedly, a firm rationalist, while Jahr expected the knowledge of the truth to come from compassion and love, and not from reason. (More recently, Bruce Jennings, professor at Vanderbilt University

[5] Cf. Fritz Jahr,'Wege zum sexualen Ethos' ['Ways to sexual ethics'], *Ethik: Sexual- und Gesellschaftsethik* 4, no. 10-11 (1928): 161-163.

[6] Cf. Fritz Jahr,'Gesinnungsdiktatur oder Gedankenfreiheit? Gedanken über eine liberale Gestaltung des Gesinnungunterrichts' ['Character dictate or freedom of thought? Thoughts about a liberal model of character education'], *Die neue Erziehung* 12 (1930): 200-202; Rinčić and Muzur,'Od bioetičara-učenika do bioetičara-učitelja' ['From bioethicist student to bioethicist teacher'].

and associate of the Hastings Center, editor-in-chief of the latest, 4th edition of (the *Encyclopaedia of*) *Bioethics*, promoted the idea of bioethical empowering of the 'common side of our existence', that is, 'membership and mutuality').[7] It could be said of Jahr's bioethics that it has a broader philosophical basis, which encompasses many European and some Far Eastern concepts, unlike Potter's, which has been built mostly on American authors. Jahr does not need a 'bridge' because, in his time, science was identified closely with the humanities. Obviously, after World War Two science diverged from the humanities, which is why Potter needed a 'bridge' to bring them together again. For Jahr, who felt a Schweitzerian reverence for life, bioethics was more abstract, timeless or omnitemporal, while Potter associated his more concrete bioethics with his own time and future. Potter definitely widened the basis of his doctrine by introducing the concept of global bioethics. One could say that the concept of integrating various perspectives, be they scientific or not, in accordance with the principles of integrative bioethics, offers a further widening of this basis. This additional philosophisation represents at the same time the descientification of bioethics. In doing this, bioethics however does not become pseudoscience but simply is not and does not want to be a 'science based on evidence' that falls into many traps. To Potter's delight, global bioethics was defined in a similar way by his Latin American colleague Daniel Otero: 'global bioethics should not be understood as a separate field of bioethics [...] but rather as an integrative perspective that puts all special aspects of bioethics and human knowledge into the context of a global project'.[8]

In an article that was sent to print in April 2001 (but was published only after Potter's death),[9] Potter commented on the plea of the Oregon professor Lubchenko for a 'new social contract for science'. A little bit like Jahr, Potter formulated here his own 'bioethical imperative', less abstract, but still insufficiently concrete to be transformed into clear standards or guidelines for acting upon: 'In the long run, global survival will not be possible if we don't bring under control and possibly reduce the world population; if we don't protect the environment; if we don't improve human health; if we don't protect

[7] Cf. Bruce Jennings,'Putting the bios back into bioethics: Prospects for health and climate justice', in *Climate Change and Health: Bioethical Insights into Values and Policy*, ed. Cheryl Cox Macpherson (New York: Springer, 2016), 34 (1-39). For Jennings' ecological-political-economical ideas, see Bruce Jennings,'Toward an ecological political economy: Accommodating nature in a new discourse of public philosophy and policy analysis', *Critical Policy Studies* 4, no. 1 (2010): 77-85, or Bruce Jennings,'Beyond the social contract of consumption: Democratic governance in the post-carbon era', *Critical Policy Studies* 4, no. 3 (2010): 222-233.

[8] Van Rensselaer Potter, e-mail to the 'Global Bioethics Network', dated 9 August 2000. DICEB *Fritz Jahr* Archive SuRi – IŠ – VRP 1.

[9] Van Rensselaer Potter,'Bridge bioethics, global bioethics, and ethical dilemmas', *Itinerarium* 10 (2002): 91-99.

biodiversity; without a transformation of society; without the sense of significance of the community'. Although these measures are not entirely concrete, their objectives are, just as is the clear call to action without which ethics would remain 'in a vacuum'.[10] Even more similar to Jahr's imperative (which also explicitly leans on Kant's imperative) is the *categorical imperative of the land ethic* (this is how J. Baird Callicott calls it,[11] while Potter calls it *Leopold's imperative*)[12] of Aldo Leopold (whose ideas are generally even closer to Jahr's than to Potters'): 'A thing is right when it tends to preserve the integrity, stability, and beauty of the biotic community. It is wrong when it tends otherwise'.[13] The Canadian environmental philosopher Laura Westra suggested in 1992 a *new categorical imperative*: 'Act so that your action will fit first (and minimally) within universal natural laws; Act so that you manifest respect and understanding acceptance of all natural processes and laws'.[14]

Bioethics, as we know, paradoxically came back to Europe not thanks to Fritz Jahr but to Potter. In June 1973, probably the first person on the continent to use the term in an article was the Italian Menico Torchio (1932-2001),[15] Professor of Ecology of the University of Pavia, who understood bioethics in the broad Potterian way, that is, not in a narrow medical sense. It turned out that in 1972 Torchio had received a book by Potter as a gift from the director of his institute, who had come back from America.[16] In the francophone world, bioethics as a term was promoted in September 1973 by Édouard Boné (1919-2006)[17] in an article in the Louvain theological journal (a centre for bioethical studies was established at Louvain Catholic University in 1983), [18] and in 1976, as is widely

[10] Potter,'Moving the culture toward more vivid utopias'.
[11] J. Baird Callicott,'Animal liberation: A triangular affair', *Environmental Ethics* 2 (1980): 311-338.
[12] Potter, *Global Bioethics*, 21.
[13] Potter, *Global Bioethics*, 20.
[14] Laura S. Westra,'The principle of 'Integrity' and *The Economy of the Earth*', *Global Bioethics* 5, no. 1 (1992): 21-30.
[15] Cf. Maurizio Mori, 'Bioethics in Italy up to 2002: An overview', in: *Bioethics and Moral Content: National Traditions of Health Care Morality*, eds. H. Tristram Engelhardt and Lisa M. Rasmussen (Dordrecht/Boston/London: Kluwer Academic Publishers, 2002), 97-120; Menico Torchio, 'Venti anni di bioetica naturalistica in Italia (1973-1993)' ['Twenty years of naturalistic bioethics in Italy (1973-1993)], in *La vita e l'uomo nell'età delle tecnologie riprtoduttive: una domanda di sapienza e di agire responsabile* [*Life and Man in the Age of Reproductive Technologies: A Question of Wisdom and Responsible Actions*], eds. Elio Sgreccia and Marinella Lombardi Ricci (Milano: Università Cattolica del Sacro Cuore, 1997), 3-6.
[16] Russo, 'Storia della bioetica' ['The history of bioethics'], 44-45.
[17] Jesuit, theologian and palaeontologist, Rector of the Faculty of Our Lady of Peace at the Belgian University of Namur.
[18] Cf. Paolo Merlo, 'Introduzione storica alla bioetica' ['A historical introduction to bioethics'], in *Dalla parte della vita – I: Itinerari di bioetica – I* [*From the side of life – I: Bioethic*

known, Europe received its first institute for bioethics – the *Borja* in Barcelona,[19] which was founded by the Jesuit, theologian, sociologist and gynaecologist-obstetrician Francesc Abel i Fabre (1933-2011), who was educated in the USA (at Georgetown, of course).[20] In England, Germany and France, bioethics took hold as a term only later (in the mid-1980s, at the same time as in Croatia thanks to Valentin Pozaić, a bishop in Zagreb).[21] With the exception of Torchio, after Boné[22] Europeans started to understand, interpret and promote bioethics in the narrow Georgetown biomedical way, often comparing it with the point of view of the Church.[23] Thus, on our continent the view became common that bioethics had been invented by Potter, but it was immediately reduced to a non-Potterian principlism. To 'return it to its right path', it was necessary to wait until the end of the century and the discovery of the work of Fritz Jahr.

---

itineraries – I] , eds. Giuseppe Zeppegno and Enrico Laghero (Cantalupa: Effatà Editrice, 2007), 11-33.

[19] The *Institut Borja de Bioètica* has been private since 1984, and since 2000 incorporated into Ramón LLull University. The institute is named after the Jesuit Francisco de Borja y Aragon (1510-1572), the third General of the Order.

[20] Cf. Sandro Spinsanti, *La bioetica: biografie per una disciplina* [*Bioethics: Biographies for a discipline*] (Milano: Franco Angeli, 1995), 21-30.

[21] Cf. Iva Rinčić and Amir Muzur, 'Variety of bioethics in Croatia: A historical sketch and a critical touch', *Synthesis Philosophica* 26, no. 2 (2011): 403-428.

[22] Édouard Boné, 'Les trois générations de la bioéthique' [The three generations of bioethics'], *Revue théologique de Louvain* 24 (1993): 478-492.

[23] Cf. Paul Favraux and Albert Chapelle, 'Bioéthique et foi chrétienne: à propos d'un livre récent' ['Bioethics and Christian faith: About a recent book'], *Nouvelle revue théologique* 108 (1986): 249-267.

BIOETHICS AND ITS DEVELOPMENTAL STAGES: BETWEEN PHILOSOPHY, SCIENCE AND RELIGION

The evolution of Potter's attitudes towards religion was very slow and complex. As early as May 1957, when he was 46 years old, Potter as an invited guest lecturer at the University of British Columbia in Vancouver, proposed a rigid attitude on evolution (in accordance with 'science based on evidence'), suggesting theologians 'examine biology and work its discoveries into their philosophy'.[1] In his address in 1962 on the occasion of the centenary of the Land Grant College Act in South Dakota, Potter pointed out three different notions of progress: religious, material, and scientific-philosophical. He said these were mutually connected and present both within society and inside the individual in different proportions. From a rather Marxist-dialectical perspective, Potter explained progress from the religious towards the material which, when it reaches the required level, turns into a new, scientific-philosophical progress (by doing so, Potter tried to separate the materialistic view from the scientific one). Reminiscent somewhat of Fritz Jahr and his insistence on reforming the educational system to provide more appropriate convictions,[2] Potter put forward the ten most important topics in education: relations between races, overpopulation, exhaustion (of resources), religious intolerance, preservation of natural resources, use of solar energy, desalinisation of the sea, freeing the creative gift, and reviewing the role of advertising in our society.[3] Potter always questioned progress, and at the end of his life, in proving the questionability of optimism related to biological evolution, he called upon Stephen Jay Gould and his *Wonderful Life*.

When it came to science, Potter always advocated self-criticism and openness towards different views. According to Potter, this is what distinguishes scientists from theologians, historians and philosophers, who can defend their own ideas without recourse to the work of their colleagues. (At a later point in time, in 1993, Potter said that some of his best works had never been quoted and that 'being right and not being quoted makes one a philosopher, if one can survive as a scientist'.)[4] The interest that Potter started showing publicly in the 1960s towards 'bridging' the gap between natural sciences on the one hand and humanities on the other took Potter (who across the USA was already perceived

---

[1] Cf. Doris, 'Land-Grant Ideology', 166-167.

[2] Cf. Jahr, 'Gesinnungsdiktatur oder Gedankenfreiheit?' ['Character dictate or freedom of thought?].

[3] Potter, 'Bridge to the future: The concept of human progress'.

[4] Van Rensselaer Potter, 'Studies on enzyme inhibition – 50 years ago', *The FASEB Journal* 7 (1993): 486-487.

as 'scientist-philosopher') to the publishing council of the *Zygon* journal of religion and science, which was started in 1966 by Ralph Burhoe, and in which Potter very soon started publishing articles.

At the time when he had already published his first book on bioethics, Potter, at the Conference on the Social Responsibility of Scientists of the New York Academy of Sciences, which was held in November 1971, put forward the view that both the Church and science had equally failed in developing ethical guidelines that could cope with the challenges of modern society, and that scientists should set up a system that would provide a timely warning of dangers emerging from the laboratory. Potter, admittedly, did not advocate direct contact with journalists, except in extraordinary situations (which he later explained in the short 'Resolution on the social responsibilities of scientists', presented at the National Academy of Sciences), or the external control of science, but it was journalists who strengthened the effect of his report by calling it a *watchdog plan*. Apart from advocating such a *Distant Early Warning* (modelled on military radar), Potter also emphasised his concern regarding the 'questionable ethics of advertising' in the field of the production and sale of drugs, cosmetics, detergents and food, where the most influential 'media promote the public taste for technology in directions that are not in the public interest'.[5] Among theologians, there were those who agreed with Potter and who were ready to admit that 'bioethics, even if it does not mention God, is a kind of theology (biotheology)'.[6]

Potter himself would maybe have not gone that far. In a dialogue with priests at Madison, he said that it would be better if people decided that God was not that almighty at all. This would lead to greater compassion towards those who suffer, but also to responsibility for our own acts. In a rather provocative way, Potter told the priests that 'we should not leave too much to God' and that 'it would be better if we returned to the idea that God is nature and that, from time to time, it is natural to hurt the innocent'.[7] With this revision of his own attitude in the direction of deism, 'intelligent design' and pantheism, Potter came closest to his role models P. Teilhard de Chardin, R. W. Emerson (whose essay 'Nature' can really be considered as pantheistic, since it celebrates Nature as an 'incarnation of thought'),[8] J. Muir (who, despite the fanatic religiosity of his

---

[5] Cf. Boyce Rensberger, 'Scientists seek a watchdog plan; system would alert public to dangers in laboratories', *New York Times*, 19 December 1971. (http://query.nytimes.com/gst/abstract.html?res=9D01E1D9173AE73ABC4152DFB467838A669EDE)

[6] Cf. Martin E. Marty and Dean A. Peerman, eds., *New Theology: No. 10* (New York: Collier Macmillan, 1973), xiv.

[7] Cf. William R. Wineke, 'Do we expect too much of God?', *Wisconsin State Journal*, 12 January 1974.

[8] Ralph Waldo Emerson, *Essays* (New York: Harper Colophon Books, 1926/1951), 400.

father, did not belong to any church),[9] and A. Leopold.[10] Love and respect towards Nature and the Earth are the characteristics of all the sources of Potter's inspiration, from Emerson, Muir and Leopold to F. Lloyd Wright's organic architecture.

In accordance with his Unitarianism, Potter advocated accepting the necessity of patience and the probabilistic aspect of existence, and was against empty words about redemption and life after death. Potter's 'humanistic theology', as it was called by the journalist and theologian William Wineke (still a very active participant in discussions about Madison religious and church questions), was aimed at improving people rather than solving their problems. Such an interpretation brings bioethics closer to those religions which (for example, Hinduism) emphasise the significance of the process (path) over the result (objective).

According to testimonies from those around him, Potter was considered an 'agnostic who turned towards practical spirituality through bioethics' (Henry Pitot, Potter's colleague and convinced Catholic) or a 'Unitarian (probably since the 1950s), and not a great churchgoer, but one of those who take their children to different churches for ecumenical and educational motives to widen their cultural horizons' (Unitarian pastor Michael Schuler). From 1962 to 1967, Potter attended every week the *Science/Christianity Ecumenical Discussion Group – Lutheran Corpus Ministry* of the Lutheran pastor Mike Teske, and was active in establishing the *Center for Advanced Study in Religion and Science*. Potter left several remarks in the margins of a mini-study that justified the establishment of this centre, signed in February 1972 by Malcolm R. Sutherland (1917-2003), the then Dean of the Meadville Theological Faculty of the Lombard College of the University of Chicago, and later Head of the Harvard Unitarian Church. Among other things, Potter suggested using a term such as 'religious beliefs', 'religious faith', 'religious values', or 'human values' instead of 'religion' in the title because, in his opinion, 'religion' had both positive and negative associations. Apart from that, Potter said that, despite the fact that he was busy, he would be willing to become a member of the centre's council.[11] Potter must have also been influenced by the article of Lynn Townsend White (1907-1987) about the historical roots of our ecological crisis, which was published in the spring of 1967 in *Science* magazine. In his article, White advocates the idea that the ecological crisis will continue to get worse until we reject the 'Christian axiom' that nature has no other reason for its existence except serving people, but also

[9] Cf. Teale, *The Wilderness World of John Muir*, xiii.
[10] Cf. Curt Meine, 'Leopold, Aldo (1887-1949)' (sic), in: *Encyclopedia of Religion and Nature*, ed. Bron Taylor (London/New York: Continuum, 2005), 1006 (1005-1008).
[11] Archive of the McArdle Laboratory, V. R. Potter, box no. 11.

that, since the roots of our problems are religious, the cure must be religious as well, 'whether we call it like that or not'.[12]

The priest M. Schuler, to whom Potter often brought his essays for his opinions, deemed Potter's thinking as being close to the *precautionary principle*.[13] It is possible that the Unitarian Church attracted Potter because it turned from science towards spiritual values (in the 1970s, just like Potter), and because of its democratic system of independent congregations, elimination of speculation about the afterworld, calm rationalism, and, most importantly, freedom of thought and openness towards other religions. Although he did not directly admit it anywhere, Potter must have been under the influence of the transcendentalism which developed in America in the early 19th century as a movement of the Unitarian reformation, which emphasised romanticist individualism and spirituality, and not only attracted Ralph Waldo Emerson (1803-1882) and Henry David Thoreau (1817-1862) but also the ecologists John Muir and Aldo Leopold. (It is interesting that the greatest authorities for the transcendentalists were Immanuel Kant (1724-1804), Friedrich Daniel Ernst Schleiermacher (1768-1834), and Indian religions, just like for Fritz Jahr.)

In any case, despite his clear position (or at least clearer than it was at the beginning of his career) that religion must accept the teaching of evolution, Potter did not deny religion but rather the practice of organised religion (and secular philosophy as well) of monopolising the right to transcendental values. 'The values embedded in the scientific ethos need to be integrated with those of religion and philosophy in order to facilitate political processes beneficial to the global environment's health'.[14] This is thinking reminiscent of the tenets of Croatian Integrative Bioethics regarding the importance of scientific and non-scientific perspectives.[15]

---

[12] Lynn White, 'The historical roots of our ecological crisis', *Science* 155, no. 3767 (1967): 1203-1207.

[13] Michael Schuler, oral communication, September 2014.

[14] Van Rensselaer Potter, 'Science, religion must share quest for global survival', *The Scientist*, 16 May 1994.

[15] On integrative bioethics, see Ante Čović, 'Integrativna bioetika i pluriperspektivizam' ['Integrative bioethics and pluri-perspectivism'], in: *Integrativna bioetika i izazovi suvremene civilizacije* [*Integrative Bioethics and the Challenges of Modern Civilisation*], ed. Velimir Valjan (Sarajevo: Bioetičko društvo u BiH, 2007), 65-75; Jurić, 'Uporišta za integrativnu bioetiku u djelu Van Rensselaera Pottera' ['The basis for integrative bioethics in the work of Van Rensselaer Potter'].

After initial discouragement with the theological ignorance of science,[16] Potter received new hope after becoming acquainted with the ideas of Hans Küng,[17] who he believed was the only theologian suggesting a way in which secular views could (and should) be integrated with traditional religious ones (unlike others – for example, the sociologist Manfred Stanley or philosopher Hans Jonas – who put survival in first place but did not go any further than that). Küng called for a 'coalition' of believers, atheists and agnostics that would lead to a world ethics.[18] However, in Potter's opinion, Küng was also wrong, just like Catholicism, Islam and so many other religions, in not understanding the danger of overpopulation and the necessity of population control.

The topic of overpopulation was a constant in Potter's intellectual work. One of the works that particularly influenced him was *The Population Bomb* of 1968 by Paul Ehrlich, a Stanford University professor of biology. Using the slogan 'While you are reading these words, four people will have died from starvation – most of them children', Ehrlich warned about the numerous dangers resulting from a lack of population control, and drafted rather naïve ways of overcoming this problem. For Ehrlich, the inalienable rights of humanity are to eat well, drink pure water, breathe clean air, live in decent uncrowded shelter, enjoy natural beauty, avoid regimentation, avoid pesticide poisoning, be free of thermonuclear war, limit families, educate our children, and have grandchildren.[19]

It is interesting that recently the debate about the relationship between religion and bioethics has been revived in a rather unusual way. In the US, people have started asking the question how it is possible that so many pioneers of bioethics were Christians (Protestants Joseph Fletcher and Paul Ramsey, Catholic Richard McCormick, and others) but that Christian bioethics has now been marginalised. Tristram Engelhardt, who accepted Orthodoxy (at the age of 50, when he took the name Herman after the missionary saint from Alaska who lived in the 18th and 19th centuries), ascribed this situation to a 'betrayal' of Christian bioethics and to the fact that everybody, even the Pope, has turned towards secular philosophy,[20] while the Catholic bioethicist Daniel Sulmasy denies this by claiming that the problem of religious bioethicists was that they relied too much

---

[16] Cf. Potter, 'Global Bioethics: Origin and development', 361; Van Rensselaer Potter and Richard Grantham, 'Scientists' responsibility for survival of the human species', *The Scientist* 6, no. 11 (1992): 10-11.

[17] Potter usually quotes: Hans Küng, *Global Responsibility: A Search for a New World Ethic* (New York: Continuum Publishing Co., 1993).

[18] Potter, 'Science, religion must share quest for global survival'.

[19] Paul R. Ehrlich, *The Population Bomb* (New York: Ballantine Books, 1968/1970).

[20] Tristram Engelhardt Jr., 'The recent history of Christian bioethics critically reassessed', *Christian Bioethics* 20, no. 2 (2014): 146-167.

on natural law, which secular bioethicists considered inevitably related to religion and therefore rejected.[21]

In an attempt to spread his theoretical basis and influence, Potter at one moment fused global bioethics with *geotherapy* by Richard Grantham, Emeritus Professor of the Claude Bernard University of Lyon, which resulted in the *Declaration for Geotherapy and Global Bioethics*, which states that: 1) Accelerating environmental degradation threatens the habitability of the biosphere. We believe that corrective action is possible and urgent. 2) Our goal is long-term survival in an acceptably maintained ecosystem. 3) We, as human beings, take full responsibility for our actions by not sacrificing natural resources for short-term gains and by working to make the world a better living place. 4) This choice will influence our biological and cultural evolution; we cannot avoid it without grave consequences. 5) A global bio-ethic should be further developed to guide and motivate geotherapy and our cultural evolution. 6) A root problem is excessive demographic growth; the earth's carrying capacity is being exceeded. With the present lifestyles and patterns of development, pollution of all kinds will increase as long as the population increases. 7) We declare that scientists should adopt the aforementioned goals and participate in meetings at all levels to apply these principals.[22]

After having formulated the main principles of global bioethics, in the 1990s Potter added the idea of an innate *fatal flaw*, by which he meant (following the example of Dobzhansky) that evolution does not take into account the long-term but rather promotes genes that take care of *here and now* survival and benefits, which results in an adaptive and flexible phenotype.[23] An example of a *fatal flaw* is the male sexual urge, which once was crucial for survival but today is the reason for overpopulation.[24] Potter advocates the idea that a *fatal flaw* should be overcome by exchanging *knowledge of the IS* with *wisdom of the OUGHT*, which would make us better, that is smarter, than natural Darwinism, enforcing (cultural) adaptation as being more effective in the long-run than selection. Towards the end of his life, Potter spoke of the work of George Kieffer from the University of Illinois in Urbana, author of the 1978 *Bioethics: A Textbook of Issues* as being particularly valuable (probably because it was actually one of the few books that abundantly quoted him). The idea of a *fatal flaw*, as in the characteristic of most people to give in to short-term pleasures and benefits, was also embraced by the Unitarian theologian Michael Schuler (Potter's acquaintance and occasional interlocutor), who reminds us of the older thinking

---

[21] Daniel P. Sulmasy, 'In defense of the amphibians: A critical appraisal of Engelhardt on the recent history of Christian bioethics', *Christian Bioethics* 20, no. 2 (2014): 187-195.

[22] Cf. Potter, 'Global Bioethics: Origin and development', 370.

[23] Cf. Van Rensselaer Potter, 'Getting to the Year 3000: Can Global Bioethics overcome evolution's fatal flaw?', *Perspectives in Biology and Medicine* 34 (1990): 89-98.

[24] Potter, 'Global Bioethics: Linking genes to ethical behavior'.

of Thomas Hobbes when stating that the 'insistent physical and emotional urge to satisfy our immediate wants prevents us from foreseeing the greater evils that necessarily attach to the goods we seek'.[25] James Gustafson, Professor of Humanities and Comparative Studies at the University of Emory in Atlanta, on the other hand, characterised Potter's optimism that global bioethics and culture will be able to overcome the evolutionary *fatal flaw* as a simplification ('*Far more than a global bioethics is required to overcome the human flaws*').[26]

In a manuscript of 1996, Van R. and Lisa A. Potter say that 'global bioethics is based on conviction (intuition, informed insight)'. In another article from the same year, Potter, even if only superficially, even falls back upon the theory of intuition of Emmanuel Levinas and Edmund Husserl, concluding that his personal opinion is that (moral) intuition is evaluated through communication with a sufficient number of broad-minded people who in one moment intuitively start to believe in the message.[27] In a third article of 1996, he wrote of global bioethics that 'it cannot be proven that it is correct, reasonable, desirable or ethical, but that it is recommended as a long-term intuition, vision or opinion'.[28] Furthermore, Van Rensselaer and Lisa Potter called upon a synergy of religions, agronomy and medicine in an attempt to affect the economy and politics and stand up against multinational *agro-corporations* and fight for a sustainable environment, revealing the particular influence of the Swedish Doctor Karl-Henrik Robèrt, founder of *The Natural Step* movement (*Det naturliga steget*, established in 1989), which fights for stability through the interaction of the economy and ecology, and strives to increase ethics through education.[29] Potter admitted that he had not realised the importance of sustainable agriculture as the core of global ethics before 1996, and that only then had he come to know about initiatives such as the Bioethical Programme of the State University in Iowa or the Declaration on Sustainability and the New Economy, and books such as Paul Hawken's *Ecology of Commerce*.[30]

Agreeing with Wallace's interpretation of religion as part of man's struggle against general entropy,[31] Potter in his *Bioethics – Bridge to the Future*

[25] Michael A. Schuler, *Making the Good Life Last: Four Keys to Sustainable Living* (San Francisco: Berrett-Koehler Publishers, Inc., 2009), 44.

[26] James M. Gustafson, 'Response to Van Rensselaer Potter, 'Getting to the year 3000: Can Global Bioethics overcome evolution's fatal flaw?", *Perspectives in Biology and Medicine* 35, no. 3 (1992): 339-344.

[27] Potter, 'What does bioethics mean?'.

[28] Potter, 'Global Bioethics: Origin and development', 364.

[29] Van Rensselaer Potter and Lisa A. Potter, 'The future of Global Bioethics: Calling on agricultural, environmental, medical, and religious ethics to address business and politics', manuscript. Archive of the McArdle Laboratory, V. R. Potter.

[30] Potter, 'What does bioethics mean?'.

[31] Anthony F. C. Wallace, *Religious Revitalization: A Function of Religion in Human History and Evolution* (Boston: Institute on Religion in an Age of Science, 1962), 24.

differentiates between the 'primitive type of religion, which includes ignorance, superstition and magic'[32] and the 'humanistic type of religion, which includes scientific humanism'.[33] The Schweitzerian idea of the need for religion as hope may have triggered Potter's acknowledgement (in his video-address, the last before his death, to the Cres-Lošinj conference in 2001) that it was 'incorrect and completely inappropriate to call bioethics a science about anything', and that he now understood bioethics as a *nature-based religion*. This idea, however, by Potter's own admission, was directly inspired by Ursula Goodenough's *religious naturalism*.[34]

When one looks at the history of the relationship between (Potter's) bioethics and philosophy, one comes to the conclusion that Potter, depending on the observer, was regarded as a 'philosopher among scientists' (the truth is that his intellectual path was influenced by Will Durant's *The Story of Philosophy*, which he received when he was fifteen) or a 'scientist among philosophers'. However, this latter label used to particularly frustrate him. After having accused the bioethicists of the Hastings Center of being non-biologists back in 1981, in 1993 he pointed out that 'the economists, political scientists, and philosophers who advise the government have never been exposed to a decent course in biology' and thus had never had the opportunity to learn that evolution is the explanation of our origin and our present.[35] Potter used to experiment with individual terms for years in order to come up with a philosophical basis that would support them better. This was also the case with the term 'global'.

Today, it is hard to be part of the scientific community without being included in global projects. Despite the development of global interactions at the end of the 20th century,[36] it remains unclear who first coined the term *global*. Unlike the history of the term *international*,[37] the origin of the word *global* is not known. What we do know is that the term appeared much earlier than its entry into everyday use (for several centuries, *globus* was synonymous with *planet*, and the adjective *global* appeared in the late 19th century meaning 'world order'). The verb *globalise* emerged in the early 20th century, at the same time as the noun

---

32 Potter's rejection of religion was moderately criticised (in her later review of Potter's first book) by Marianna Gensabella Furnari, 'The scientist demanding wisdom: The 'Bridge to the Future' by Van Rensselaer Potter', *Perspectives in Biology and Medicine* 45, no. 1 (2002): 40 (31-42).

33 Potter, *Bioethics: Bridge to the Future*, 85.

34 Potter, 'The intellectual 'last will'', 150.

35 Van Rensselaer Potter, 'Emeritus professors can, assistant professors mustn't', *The FASEB Journal* 7 (1993): 255-256.

36 J. A. Scholte, *What is Globalization? The Definitional Issue – Again* (Coventry: Department of Politics and International Studies, University of Warwick, 2002) (http://www.csgr.org), 4.

37 J. Bentham, *An Introduction to the Principles of Morals and Legislation* (Kitchener: Batoche Books, 1781/2000).

globalism. Finally, *globality*, as a state, came into use only recently and its meaning is close to but not identical with *globalisation* (as a trend).[38] According to Schott, it seems that a degree of (scientific) globality has emerged during the process of globalisation.[39] With McLuhan's concept of a 'global village',[40] different concepts of globality, globalisation and globalism appeared[41] and spread across disciplines and definitions, as well as political contexts, which has also happened with bioethics.

The fact is that Fritz Jahr's teaching in our time has become globalised by spreading it, though not with its original intent but rather as a reaction to the pushiness of Georgetown bioethics in the late 20th century. Fritz Jahr's ethics was, in a way, global. Educated in the strict tradition of Pietism, Jahr was an expert on the Bible and a passionate reader influenced by an array of sources from different countries and cultures – German (Kant, Schleiermacher, Bregenzer, Basedow, Goethe, Hartmann, Hebbel, Herder, Krause, Wagner, etc.), English (Darwin and Wesley), Russian (Tolstoy), French (Montaigne and Rousseau), Danish (Andersen), Spanish (Abel), Greek (Socrates), Italian (Boccaccio, Casanova), etc.[42] In one of his 22 articles, Fritz Jahr showed that he was also familiar with the basic philosophies of the Far East. Maybe under the influence of Arthur Schopenhauer (whom he had read in 1926), Jahr, in an article in the *Kosmos* magazine of January 1927, recognised that 'India indeed fertilised the spiritual life of Europe, as had Germany as its then most important territory, although only in the time of Romanticism', and quoted Buddha (especially the *Jataka* tales) and the Indian philosopher, biologist, archaeologist and writer Jagdish Chandra Bose (1858-1937), as well as the traditions of sankhya and yoga. A particular difference which Fritz Jahr notices between the Indian philosophy of worshiping life and the European attempts to protect plants through legal regulation lies in the fact that in Europe 'if a plant is present in abundance, the state does not think about protecting it for its own sake'.[43]

---

[38] Scholte, *What is Globalization?*

[39] T. Schott, 'The world scientific community: Globality and globalisation', *Minerva* 29, no. 4 (1991): 440 (440-461).

[40] M. McLuhan, *The Gutenberg Galaxy: The Making of Typographic Man* (Toronto: University of Toronto Press, 1962).

[41] Mislav Kukoč, 'Introduction: Philosophy and globalization I', *Synthesis philosophica* 47, no. 1 (2009), 3 (3-5).

[42] Iva Rinčić and Amir Muzur, 'Fritz Jahr: The invention of bioethics and beyond', *Perspectives in Biology and Medicine* 54, no. 4 (2011): 550-556; Rinčić and Muzur, *Fritz Jahr i rađanje europske bioetike* [*Fritz Jahr and the Emergence of European Bioethics*], 45-62.

[43] Fritz Jahr, 'Bio-Ethik: eine Umschau über die ethischen Beziehungen des Menschen zu Tier und Pflanze' ['Bio-ethics: Reviewing the ethical relations of humans towards animals and plants'] , *Kosmos* 24, no. 1 (1927): 2-4.

Fifty years later, 'global' must have had a significantly different meaning for Van Rensselaer Potter. According to Potter, global bioethics should unite medical bioethics (with its short-term perspective) and ecological ethics (with its long-term perspective)[44] and attempt to 'balance the morality of decisions in health care with decisions involving the environment',[45] thus 'fixing' the gap created by Georgetown bioethicists (especially T. Beauchamp, J. Childress, R. Veatch and others). For Potter, the 'global' is expected to 'transcend the dichotomy between science and religion'[46] by providing a 'secular source of moral authority in a dialogue with religions that are ready to collaborate'.[47] (Potter criticised the speech of Vaclav Havel which he, when receiving the Medal of Freedom in Philadelphia in 1994, concluded by calling for a return to God.)[48]

However, it would be wrong to neglect the other, deeper aspects (or developmental phases) of Potter's globality. First, Van Rensselaer Potter started from the concept of the *land*, which was put forward by Aldo Leopold, whose mystical vision of nature Potter merged with his own idea of the 'second level', the *Earth* which, again, was probably coined under the influence of the ideas of Alan Gregg and Norman J. Berrill and the tradition of Earth Day. Moreover, it should be remembered that Potter embraced the Spencerian biologistic analogy between the Earth and human organism as a variant of his favourite analogy between the micro and macro world.[49] Following these 'signposts', it is not difficult to reach the concept of 'global'. However, for Potter, apart from these unifying and transcending characteristics, globality had to subsume at least two more aspects. First, for scientists frustrated by being ignored by Washington's Kennedy Institute of Ethics and New York's Hastings Center, 'global' could mean, as already mentioned, 'not-only-American', that is, international. Indeed, was it not Potter who developed and fostered a worldwide network of followers and admirers in South America, Europe and Asia?[50] Second, as Potter says, apart from encompassing the basic studies of behavioural genetics and ethical decisions on the care for human health and the Earth, 'global' for him meant making decisions at the world level.[51] Oriented towards medicine and the environment, Potter's global bioethics also deals with universal – that is, global – problems, particularly those that concern Potter's main obsession,

---

[44] Potter, *Global Bioethics*, 7; cf. also Van Rensselaer Potter, 'Aldo Leopold's land ethic revisited: Two kinds of bioethics', *Perspectives in Biology and Medicine* 30, no. 2 (1987): 159 (157-169).

[45] Van Rensselaer Potter, 'Global Bioethics as a secular source of moral authority for long-term human survival', *Global Bioethics* 5, no. 1 (1992): 5-11.

[46] Potter, *Global Bioethics*, 68.

[47] Potter, 'Global Bioethics as a secular source'.

[48] Potter, 'Global Bioethics: Origin and development', 361-363.

[49] Cf. Potter, *Global Bioethics*, 34.

[50] Potter, 'The intellectual, last will'.

[51] Potter, 'Global Bioethics: Linking genes to ethical behavior'.

overpopulation, a typical global environmental issue which involves the depletion of natural resources (soil, water, wood, etc.) In Potter's own words, 'global bioethics touches on many aspects of the world crisis'.[52] It is known that Potter studied and appreciated the ideas of Wallace Stegner, Garrett Hardin, Eugene P. Odum, Richard Falk, Barry Commoner, Paul Shepard, Lester Brown (environmental evolution), Richard Grantham (geotherapy) and others, some of who went so far as to compare the human population with a 'cancer of the planet'. Potter was familiar with the problem of overpopulation in Ethiopia from the work of Lloyd Timberlake, and overpopulation in South America from William Vogt, who was also strongly influenced by Aldo Leopold, Homer L. Shantz, and Isaiah Bowman.

Of course, Potter's global bioethics found new life and received the strongest support in the promotional activities of the Florentine anthropologist Brunetto Chiarelli, author of the book *Bioetica globale* [*Global Bioethics*] (1993) and editor-in-chief of the *Global Bioethics* journal (1988-1991 *Problemi di bioetica* [*Bioethical Problems*]). Chiarelli spoke about *relaunching* Potter's global bioethics but without mentioning where and when one should look for the beginnings of global bioethics.[53] It is possible that Chiarelli was recognising Potter's own admission that 'the concept, but not the name, of global bioethics [...] was born in the course of a lecture at the South Dakota State University [in 1962]'.[54] In the same article, Potter also mentions that 'the term *global bioethics* [was] employed for the first time in my [Potter's] 1988 book by that name.'[55]

Global bioethics as a new discipline strives for a pact between Humanity and Nature to ensure humans' survival on the Earth.[56] According to Chiarelli, Potter was not alone in his endeavours. 'This is why Van Rensselaer Potter and I established the *Global Bioethics* journal and I wrote the book *Bioetica globale* (1995), which attests to a naturalist and anthropological distinction of bioethics with respect to moral philosophy, medical deontology, and environmental ethics'.[57] In a more recent article,[58] Chiarelli suggests adding two more names to

---

[52] Van Rensselaer Potter, 'Global Bioethics facing a world in crisis', *Global Bioethics* 5, no. 1 (1992): 69-76.

[53] Brunetto Chiarelli, 'Man, nature and ethics: Global Bioethics', *Global Bioethics* 5, no. 1 (1992): 13-20; Brunetto Chiarelli, *Bioetica globale* [*Global Bioethics*] (Firenze: Angelo Pontecorboli, 1993), 179.

[54] Potter, 'Global Bioethics as a secular source'.

[55] Ibid.

[56] For Potter's reflections on survival, see for example: Van Rensselaer Potter, 'Bioethics and the human prospect: The meaning of survival', *Wisconsin Medical Alumni Quarterly* 23, no. 4 (1983): 19.

[57] Brunetto Chiarelli, 'Global Bioethics: A suggested distinction between ethic and morality', in *Implementing Ecological Integrity: Restoring Regional and Global Environmental and Human Health*, eds. P. Crabbé, A. J. Holland, L. Ryszkowski and L. Westra (Dordrecht: Springer, 2000), 358 (351-360).

the story of the emergence of global bioethics as the 'scientific formulations of globalised opinion that was promoted in the 1980s': Antonio Moroni and Laura Westra.[59]

In his presentation held on 6 November 1991 in Trento (where he was a guest at the Italian Congress of Anthropologists headed by B. Chiarelli), Potter introduced a thought by a Benedictine monk from Vallombrosa from the beginning of the 19th century (whose work he had discovered through a translation by Menico Torchi, who had drawn his attention to it) into the story of the development of his own environmental ethics, and dated the beginning of his definitive concept of bioethics to 1975. This is when he, in his presidential address to the American Association for Cancer Research, schematically outlined bioethics as a combination of biological knowledge and knowledge of the system of human values, and then divided it into medical (with a short-term perspective) and ecological (with a long-term view) bioethics. In his presentation, in which he, logically and as expected, tried to give greater significance to anthropology, Potter depicted global bioethics as being comprehensive, and, by alluding to M. Mead's old ideas about 'Chairs of the Future', proposed the establishment of 'Institutes of Global Bioethics and Global Biotechnology' at universities around the world, which could all be financed for the price of the 284 *Tomahawk* missiles that had been fired during the Gulf War. According to Potter, the tasks of global bioethics are to limit the human population, preserve human dignity, preserve the ecosystem, and eliminate diseases and weapons of mass destruction, a process that involves humility, interdisciplinary competence, global responsibility, compassion, and justice. For Potter, global bioethics is necessary for survival, but not just any kind of survival, as survival can be miserable, plain, idealistic, irresponsible or acceptable.[60]

During its dynamic development over the last few decades, bioethics has faced various issues: bioethics for whom?;[61] why has bioethics become so boring?;[62] and finally, is there one or more bioethics?[63] One of the questions that the historians of bioethics and epistemologists will have to answer (or at least deal with) is the question of the definition and the scope of the 'globality' of

---

58 Brunetto Chiarelli, 'The bioecological bases of Global Bioethics', *Global Bioethics* 25, no. 1 (2014): 19-26.

59 Ibid., 19.

60 Van Rensselaer Potter, 'Global Bioethics – Bridge to the future, bridge to peace', lecture at the Italian Congress of Anthropology, Trento, 6 November 1991.

61 Potter, 'Bioethics for whom?'.

62 Jonsen, 'Why has bioethics become so boring?'.

63 H. Tristram Engelhardt, 'Introduction: Bioethics as a global phenomenon', in *The Annals of Bioethics: Regional Perspectives in Bioethics*, eds. J. F. Peppin and M. J. Cherry (London/New York: Taylor and Francis, 2008), xiii (xiii-xxii).

global bioethics. As has been shown here, the globality of the ideas of Fritz Jahr is based on Jahr's turning towards non-European countries, especially Indian philosophical concepts and thinkers, which is indeed congruent with Van Rensselaer Potter's attempt to 'decentralise' (American) bioethics. However, Potter's globality, besides being explicit and crucial, proved to be a deeper concept merging Leopold's legacy of land ethics with concern for the Earth and the intentional internationalisation of bioethical environmental and medical issues.[64]

Just as the integrativity of integrative bioethics is interpreted in so many different ways (cf. the Krakow model, Stephen Sodeke, Michael Tai, etc.), so has the globality introduced by Potter also been understood in different ways. Henk ten Have, for example, connected Potter's globality with the 'global community', an expression which, according to ten Have, could be explained in three different ways: (1) a diachronic use, including past, present, and future generations, (2) a synchronic ecological use, including non-human species, and (3) a synchronic planetary use, including all human beings worldwide.[65]

However, Potter did not just restrict himself to global bioethics. His ethics was to have encompassed *land ethics*, *wildlife ethics*, *population ethics* and *consumption ethics*.[66] According to P. Whitehouse, Potter was also thinking about *privilege bioethics*,[67] which he said in his video address to the participants of the Tokyo conference in 1998 was the 'ethics of care of the too privileged for the least privileged' in accordance with the French concept of *noblesse oblige* of 1808.[68] In the mid-1980s, that is immediately before conceiving 'global bioethics', Potter, in polemics with Clements, spoke about *medical bioethics* as a reconciliation of medical ethics and environmental bioethics.[69] In the summer of 1994, Potter wanted to propose a *real bioethics*, which would be both 'true and realistic' (that is, a biocentrism which is actually an enlightened or realistic anthropocentrism combined with a humanism that takes into account the needs, interests and well-being of people. Something similar was suggested by the

---

[64] An analysis of Jahr's and Potter's globality is provided by the article: Amir Muzur and Iva Rinčić, 'Two kinds of globality: A comparison of Fritz Jahr and Van Rensselaer Potter's bioethics', *Global Bioethics* 26, no. 1 (2015): 23-27.

[65] Henk ten Have, 'Global Bioethics and communitarianism', *Theoretical Medicine and Bioethics* 32, no. 5 (2011): 315-326.

[66] Cf. Giovanni Russo, 'Un rapporto sulla bioetica dai pionieri' ['A report on bioethics by its pioneers'], in *Bilancio di venticinque anni di bioetica* [*A report on twenty-five years of bioethics*], ed. Giovanni Russo (Torino: Editrice Elle, 1997), 5-24.

[67] Whitehouse, 'The rebirth of bioethics: Extending the original formulations of Van Rensselaer Potter', W27.

[68] *Script for a Videotape for Tokyo*, 6.

[69] Colleen D. Clements, ''Therefore choose life': Reconciling medical and environmental bioethics', *Perspectives in Biology and Medicine* 28, no. 3 (1985): 407-425; Potter, 'A response to Clements'.

environmental ethics theoretician Paul Taylor).[70] However, he did not go through with this idea. In a manuscript entitled *Origin and development of Real Bioethics*, dated 13 September 1994, he struck through the word *real* and replaced it with *global* and added a remark in the margin: '*Hold before retyping – we'll see what Cothern comes up with*', as well as an instruction that the manuscript was to be sent to the Rector and Andrew Jameton[71] (from the University of Nebraska in Omaha). Potter obviously had the intention of adjusting the text for Richard Cothern, editor of the *Handbook for Environmental Risk Decision Making* (at that time still in preparation, and published in 1996 with Potter's article on the origin and development of GLOBAL bioethics).[72] This is how *real bioethics* was 'postponed' until 1996.[73] In a manuscript from the second half of the 1990s, Potter said that the term *real bioethics* (meaning 'comprehensive applied ethics') was necessary since Hellegers 'apparently without knowing the goals set up in 1970-1971', a few months later had defined bioethics 'in terms of hard clinical decisions for doctors and patients'.[74] Actually, it seems that Potter with the invention of *real bioethics* only wanted to artificially distance it from *environmental ethics* as the 'traditional ethics of pure reason'. Just as those from the Kennedy Institute of Ethics at that time had taken over the medical-ethics part of bioethics, Potter feared that the philosophers from the Hastings Center would usurp the environmental part of global bioethics (and bridge ethics too, although Potter did not actually have to change the name at all, as the concept was not changed significantly). For the formulation of this 'new' *real bioethics*, Potter felt particularly obliged to Aldo Leopold, but – totally unexpectedly – also to another Wisconsin Unitarian (and Leopold's acquaintance), Max Carl Otto (1876-1968), born in Saxony, and Professor of Philosophy from 1908 to 1947 at the University of Wisconsin in Madison, who as a big supporter of James' and Dewey's pragmatism became known for the idea that 'morality is a means for the satisfaction of human wants'. It is not clear how Otto could ever be identified with the subtlety of Leopold's (and even Potter's) abstract love for nature. His reflections are closer to the opposite. It seems that Potter, however, in another of his rather superficial readings, wanted to point to Otto's

70 Paul W. Taylor, *Respect for Nature: A Theory of Environmental Ethics* (Princeton: Princeton University Press, 1986); cf. also J. Baird Callicott, 'Environmental Ethics: I. overview', in: *Encyclopedia of Bioethics*, vol. 2, 3rd edition, ed. Stephen Post (New York: Macmillan Reference USA, 2004), 757-769.

71 Jameton published his article 'Global Bioethics' in 1994, *Cambridge Quarterly of Healthcare Ethics* 3, no. 3 (1994): 449-466.

72 Potter, 'Global Bioethics: Origin and development', 359-373.

73 Van Rensselaer Potter, 'Real Bioethics: Biocentric or anthropocentric?', *Ethics and the Environment* 1, no. 2 (1996): 177-183.

74 Van Rensselaer Potter, 'Real Bioethics: A comprehensive applied ethics for long-term acceptable survival', manuscript. Archive of the McArdle Laboratory, V. R. Potter. On the first page, Potter wrote by hand: 'sent to *Academic Press* (Bentley) and rejected'.

anthropocentrism as enlightened and nature-conscious, which again resulted in confusion.

At the end of his life, Potter made an attempt with *Life Ethics* too, which he mentioned in the introductory statement on the occasion of the establishment of the Global Bioethics Society[75] (after giving up the term *international* in the name, Potter turned towards regional global bioethics, but already in the same month – July 1999 – the Society was renamed as the International Council of Global Bioethics),[76] and then also with *Deep Global Bioethics*, whose task was to 'view the essence of human thoughts and deeds, adding passion and spirit to our relationship with nature'. Only a few articles were published on this topic: one in 1998 with Potter as co-author,[77] and the others as the work of Peter Whitehouse.[78] In his address to the participants of the Tokyo congress in 1998, Potter said that he 'believed that [Whitehouse] sees *Deep Bioethics* as a dimension which questions bioethics more deeply than pure empiricism, calling for an internal differentiation between right and wrong that is not easy to quantify'.[79] Whitehouse recognised that Potter had returned to global bioethics, although, according to Whitehouse, deep bioethics, because of the introduction of intuition and spirituality, represented a bigger challenge.[80] That year, 1998, the term *bridge bioethics* started to be used in order to point out the evolution of the concept of the original Potterian idea from the 1970s and its later phases.[81]

In fact, *deep bioethics* was a not particularly original version of the *deep ecology* (*ecosophy*) that was promoted by the Norwegian philosopher Arne Dekke Eide Næss (1912-2009).[82] Strongly influenced by Rachel Carson, Aldo Leopold and Gandhi, Næss advocated a *deep ecology* as opposed to the prevailing *shallow ecology*. Næss first used the term *deep ecology* in 1972-1973 in his article 'The shallow and the deep: Long-range ecology movement', and by *deep* he meant asking '*why* and *how*' where others did not. For example, ecology as science does not ask what kind of society would be best for the preservation of a specific

---

[75] Van Rensselaer Potter, e-mail to the 'Global Bioethics Network', dated 1 July 1999. DICEB *Fritz Jahr* Archive SuRi – IŠ – VRP 1.

[76] Van Rensselaer Potter, e-mail to the 'Global Bioethics Network', dated 21 July 1999. DICEB *Fritz Jahr* Archive SuRi – IŠ – VRP 1.

[77] Van Rensselaer Potter and Peter J. Whitehouse, 'Deep and Global Bioethics for a liveable Third Millennium', *The Scientist* 12 (1998): 1-9.

[78] Cf. Peter Whitehouse, 'Toward a deeper bioethics', *Minding Nature* 3, no. 3 (2010), 18-24.

[79] *Script for a Videotape for Tokyo*, 7.

[80] Whitehouse, 'The rebirth of bioethics', W27.

[81] Cf. Van Rensselaer Potter, 'Bioethics, biology, and the biosphere: Fragmented ethics and 'Bridge Bioethics'', *Hastings Center Report* 29, no. 1 (1999): 38-40.

[82] A passionate mountaineer and Norwegian Green Party candidate, he was the youngest full professor of the University of Oslo of all time. Later, he taught at the University of Hong Kong.

ecosystem.[83] This *deep questioning* brought Næss to two 'final norms' or 'intuitions': *self-realisation* (meaning the spiritual achievement of an individual) and *biocentric equality* (the right to life and development of all the elements of the biosphere).[84] With George Sessions,[85] Næss in 1984 formulated the *principles of deep ecology*: 1) The well-being and flourishing of human and non-human Life on Earth have value in themselves; 2) Richness and diversity of life forms contribute to the realization of these values and are also values in themselves; 3) Humans have no right to reduce this richness and diversity except to satisfy *vital* needs; 4) The flourishing of human life and cultures is compatible with a substantial decrease of the human population; the flourishing of non-human life requires such a decrease; 5) Present human interference with the non-human world is excessive, and the situation is rapidly worsening; 6) Policies must therefore be changed; 7) The ideological change is mainly that of appreciating life quality (dwelling in situations of inherent value) rather than adhering to an increasingly higher standard of living; and 8) Those who subscribe to the foregoing points have an obligation directly or indirectly to try to implement the necessary changes.[86] Just like Leopold, Næss was also attacked by some – Al Gore, for example – for his 'misanthropic ecocentrism'.

Potter's (or equally Whitehouse's) *deep bioethics* was unable to leave a deep impression. While even the first term, *bioethics*, had still not been unambiguously interpreted or accepted, another one had already appeared – *global bioethics*, and then, a few years later, a third one (*deep bioethics*) and a fourth one (*real bioethics*). The author is no longer among us to explain why it was necessary to change the name (except if it was for marketing reasons and mere aspiration to originality). Of course, now and then someone will appear who will notice an outline of logic in this sequence, such as the young Colombian assistant A. M. Wilches Flórez, who noticed that Potter modelled his basic bioethical thought under the influence of the people whom he was talking

---

[83] Bill Devall and George Sessions, eds., *Deep Ecology: Living as if Nature Mattered* (Salt Lake City/Layton: Gibbs M. Smith, Inc. / Peregrine Smith Books, 1985), 65.

[84] Cf. Arne Næss, 'The deep ecological movement: Some philosophical aspects', in: *Deep Ecology for the 21st Century: Readings on the Philosophy and Practice of the New Environmentalism*, ed. George Sessions (Boston/London: Shambala, 1995), 64-84.

[85] Philosopher of the Sierra College in Rocklin in California who particularly appreciates J. Muir, H. D. Thoreau, D. H. Lawrence, Robinson Jeffers, Theodore Roszak, L. Mumford, G. Orwell and A. Huxley, but also Taoism and Zen. Cf. George Sessions, 'Ecocentrism and the anthropocentric detour', in: *Deep Ecology for the 21st Century: Readings on the Philosophy and Practice of the New Environmentalism*, ed. George Sessions (Boston/London: Shambala, 1995), 156-183.

[86] Devall and Sessions, *Deep Ecology*, 70.

to or by what he was reading at the time (P. Whitehouse, H. Küng or H. Sakamoto),[87] but it is to be expected that this will go unnoticed.

[87] Ángela Maria Wilches Flórez, 'La propuesta bioética de Van Rensselaer Potter, cuatro décadas después' ['The bioethical proposal of Van Rensselaer Potter four decades later], *Opción* 27, no. 66 (2011): 70-84.

IN PLACE OF AN AFTERWORD: POTTER AFTER POTTER

Potter's personal bioethical development can be divided into four phases:

1) 1956-1966: involvement in issues in the relationship between science and society, and also religion and science;

2) 1966-1975: enthusiasm surrounding the focus on and launch of bridge bioethics, media and academic engagement and publications;

3) 1975-1987: disenchantment with the domination of Georgetown, bitterness and frustration;

4) 1987-2001: newfound enthusiasm – turning towards Aldo Leopold, 'departure' from the USA and the creation of an international network, and the emergence and promotion of global bioethics and also other versions (deep, real).

Just by looking at these phases, it is clear that for most of his life Potter was not lacking in creative or entrepreneurial spirit. As an emeritus professor, Potter argued that it was precisely professors who should be making the greatest contribution, as in the earlier parts of their careers they are constrained by ambitions of advancement and the need to obtain funding and projects.[1] He was afraid of neither authority nor taking action. In March 1992, he wrote to the Mayor of Madison Paul Soglin (who is today once again mayor),[2] informing him that he had ordered five copies of the book *State of the World 1992*, and that every city councillor and the head of each city service should familiarise themselves with the eighth chapter of the book, which is entitled 'Shaping cities'. Potter offered to personally take a copy of the book to the mayor's house. (It is interesting that he sent a copy of his e-mail to the mayor to the main newspapers: *The Wisconsin State Journal* and *The Capitol Times*.) He also dreamt of teaching Pope John Paul II about the biological nature of people and using the Pope's influence to rid the world of misery.[3]

The development of the international Global Bioethics Network, which brought together some forty of Potter's followers, perhaps initially seemed something of a desperate move but later proved to be a crucial guarantee of the spreading of

---

1 Potter, 'Emeritus Professors'; A. J. S. Rayl, 'Emeritus status offers some distinguished faculty a chance to parlay investigations on higher level', *The Scientist*, 9 November 1992. (http:www.the-scientist.com/?articles.view/articleNo/12553/title/Emeritus-Status…).

2 Soglin is known as the first mayor and fourth politician from the US to meet Fidel Castro (1975), and was a supporter of the previously mentioned *Monona Terrace* project.

3 Trosko, 'Scientific concepts of human nature'.

Potter's doctrine and its survival after his departure. This somewhat financially demanding but often strong institutionalisation of teaching is necessary in all cases that concern ideas that have strong lobbies set against them that control journals and institutions (especially educational ones). Similar 'rescues' and initial (and maybe even later) dark periods have been experienced by many religions. This was the case with psychoanalysis, thanks to Freud's followers who were responsible for missionary propagation in certain countries (Ferenczi in Hungary, Weiss in Italy, etc.), and also on a smaller scale in integrative bioethics, which has survived in South-East Europe with support in Slovenia, Croatia, Bosnia and Herzegovina, Serbia, Macedonia, Bulgaria and Albania.

One of Potter's characteristics was that he was completely conscious of the pursuit of originality, which among other things manifested itself in the coining of new words. Besides 'bioethics', whose use (as opposed to Fritz Jahr's use of it) is rather clumsy and linguistically inconsistent, in about 1941 Potter came up with the terms 'homogenate' and 'homogenisator',[4] and in around 1969 *litterbird* (a person who collects litter in contrast with the English expression *litterbug* for a person who drops it). His followers came up with new words too. J. Trosko is responsible for 'epigenetic toxicology', Masahiro Morioka (the first Japanese follower of Potter) came up with 'life studies' and 'philosophy of life', P. Whitehouse, as we have seen, 'deep bioethics', and Potter's inspiration Waddington supplied 'epigenotype' and 'epigenetic', while the Croatian school of integrative bioethics has also been attacked for the coining of neologisms.

One of the most intriguing questions in the history of bioethics is why Potter remained so systematically marginalised in the USA for such a long time. Philosophers naturally ignored him as a biologist, and Georgetown biologists viewed him as competition. Moreover, the position of the Kennedy Institute towards Potter and his work from the beginning right up to the present has been to deny his importance, with 'misses' given more prominence than any opportunities. The official website of the Institute makes no mention of Potter,[5] and his works are not to be found on the shelves of the Institute's library.[6] Oxford University Press have adopted a similar position, and in the majority of the works that they have published on bioethics (and there are plenty of them), [7]

---

[4] Cf. Doris, 'Land-Grant Ideology', 263.

[5] Cf. https://kennedyinstitute.georgetown.edu/about/news/kie40th-hist.cfm.html

[6] Of course, Potter's works are held in other Georgetown University libraries. For example, *Bioethics: Bridge to the Future* and *Global Bioethics* can be found at the Lauinger Library (named after an alumnus who died in the Vietnam War), which is situated about a kilometre north-east of the Kennedy Institute, and some copies are located outside the campus.

[7] Cf., for example: Akira Akabayashi, ed., *The Future of Bioethics: International Dialogues* (Oxford: Oxford University Press, 2014) deals exclusively with topics concerning medical ethics; or Roger Crisp, ed., *The Oxford Handbook of the History of Ethics* (Oxford: Oxford

they either do not mention Potter or marginalise his role,[8] while in a large number of publications they do not distinguish between medical ethics and bioethics.[9] On the other hand, there are those who after reading Potter changed their opinions. Irina Pollard called her book *Bioscience Ethics*,[10] but increasingly came under the influence of Potter, thus widening her own horizons.[11]

In his work on the history of American medical ethics, which goes back to the 'bioethics revolution' of the 1970s, the philosopher Robert Baker completely ignores Potter. According to Baker, the reason for the emergence (and initial success and rise) of bioethics was the disenchantment with and ignorance of medical ethics in the USA, which reminds Baker of the story of the success of *Coca Cola* following the prohibition, sale and consumption of alcohol in the first half of the 20th century. During the 1960s, bureaucrats, lawyers, philosophers and others had entered the sphere of medical ethics with the result that it had stopped being medical.[12]

The *enfant terrible* of bioethics, the Texan doctor of medicine and philosopher Hugo Tristram Engelhardt Jr. (1941-2018), in his *The Foundations of Bioethics* of 1986, similarly does not mention Potter's name anywhere, and sees bioethics as a lingua franca in a world concerned with health but which does not have a common ethical standpoint or an 'open, peaceful discussion between various groups, such as atheists, Catholics, Jews, Protestants, Marxists, heterosexuals and homosexuals, on matters of public health policy'.[13] It is no wonder that Potter, in the pages of his copy of Engelhardt's book, everywhere wrote 'and the environment', irritatedly circling the mentioning of Daniel Callahan, and in one place adding 'words, words, words'.

University Press, 2013), where bioethics is mentioned only twice in passing in observations on the ethics of Cynicism and Stoicism.

[8] Such an approach can be seen, for example, in Jessica Pierce and George Randels, *Contemporary Bioethics: A Reader with Cases* (New York: Oxford University Press, 2010), 2 and 661, where it is admitted that Potter was the first to use the term 'bioethics' but with an incorrect derivation from 'bios'. George H. Kieffer, *Bioethics: A Textbook of Issues* (Reading, MA: Addison-Wesley Publishing Co., 1979), 359 and 371 says that Potter was 'one of the first to use the term 'bioethics', and in another place that it was Potter who proposed the name of a new discipline, etc.

[9] When the authors of this book proposed a popularisation work on the topic of bioethics for the Oxford University Press *Very Short Introductions* series, they were rejected with the excuse that there already existed *A Very Short Introduction to Medical Ethics*.

[10] Irina Pollard, *Bioscience Ethics* (New York: Cambridge University Press, 2009).

[11] Cf. Lainie Friedman Ross, 'Forty years later: The scope of bioethics revisited', *Perspectives in Biology and Medicine* 53, no. 3 (2010): 452-457.

[12] Robert Baker, *Before Bioethics: A History of American Medical Ethics from the Colonial Period to the Bioethics Revolution* (New York: Oxford University Press, 2013), 274-308.

[13] H. Tristram Engelhardt, Jr., *The Foundations of Bioethics* (New York/Oxford: Oxford University Press, 1986), 5.

In the 1988 collection *Bioethics in the USA*, the editor Hans-Martin Sass also fails to mention Potter's name or works, and generally identifies bioethics with medical ethics. Among the fixed points in the development of bioethics, one can find the establishment of the Hastings Center and Kennedy Institute, the launching of the journals of these two institutions, the publication of the *Encyclopedia of Bioethics*, and the organisation of committees and symposia, but not the work of Potter.[14]

Sociologist Tina Stevens, in her classic 2000 work on the history of bioethics in the USA attributes the emergence of the bioethics movement to a social critique of science characteristic of the post-war period in America and the traditional American ambivalence towards progress. Despite the fact that Potter was among the most vocal of these critics of science and that it was he who publicly relativised (pragmatically) the idea of progress, Stevens fails to mention Potter in her book.[15] (In fact, Tina Stevens barely mentions the Kennedy Institute of Ethics in Georgetown but dedicates an entire chapter to the 'leader of leaders': the Hastings Center.)

One would not even expect to find Potter in the *Story of Bioethics*, which was published by Georgetown University in 2003. However, in fact, he is mentioned twice in an article by W. Reich, and more than just in passing. However, the other authors, important names in bioethics, E. D. Pellegrino, T. L. Beauchamp, J. F. Childress, R. M. Veatch, H. T. Engelhardt, C. E. Curran, L. S. Cahill, W. F. May, P. A. King and L. Walters, did not find a place in their memories and reflections for the person who first used the term 'bioethics' and who, over three decades, turned it into a complex discipline.[16]

The medical sociologist Renée Fox and medical historian Judith Swazey, who in their 2008 monograph *Observing Bioethics* agree with the compromise of Reich's theory of the idea of bioethics being born in two places: first with Potter, and then a little later with Hellegers and Shriver, mention Potter twice in their book, but more in passing. Although they do not ignore the Hastings Center, Fox and Swazey, in contrast to Stevens, dedicate a chapter exclusively to the Kennedy Institute of Ethics. Nevertheless, the authors succeed in looking beyond the Americocentric horizon and have a chapter devoted to 'bioethics circling the globe', as well as ones on the development of bioethics in France and Pakistan (although precisely why these places is not clear). Naturally, when discussing bioethics in the world, the authors display a somewhat superficial

[14] Hans-Martin Sass, ed., *Bioethik in den USA: Methoden, Themen, Positionen* [*Bioethics in the USA: Methods, Themes, Positions*] (Berlin/Heidelberg/New York/London/Paris/Tokyo: Springer-Verlag, 1988), 36.
[15] Stevens, *Bioethics in America*.
[16] Jennifer K. Walter and Eran P. Klein, eds., *The Story of Bioethics: From Seminal Works to Contemporary Explorations* (Washington: Georgetown University Press, 2003).

knowledge of trends, which, in part, they recognise. Seemingly unfamiliar with (and not citing) Potter's book on global bioethics, they offer a recipe for how to 'internationalise international bioethics', i.e. by undertaking detailed studies of bioethics, and its development and problems in individual cultures in order to create a bioethic/bioethics that would meet different needs.[17] Such a partial, and theoretically and methodologically not particularly original 'review of American bioethics' approach was seen in the 1990s in the European attempt to develop its own principles, which did not meet with success.

Equally as 'generously' as by Fox and Swazey, Potter's contribution is covered by one of the first historians of bioethics (American, of course, although he does dedicate 4 out of more than 400 pages of his book to bioethics elsewhere), Albert Jonsen (born 1931). Educated in a very Catholic environment, in his 1998 book *The Birth of Bioethics*, Jonsen cites certain European sources and mentions Potter twice. The first time is when discussing the birth of the name of the discipline (he does not choose between Shriver, Potter and Hellegers, although he concludes that Potter's vision was broader and that Hellegers confined himself to biomedical issues), while the second is when Potter's understanding of the prefix *bio-* is seen theologically (which in fact is not true, since Potter took *bio-* from biological science and not like theologians from the Greek *bios*).[18] Jonsen always stresses that the start of bioethics should be considered the publication of an article on the Seattle dialysis dilemma in *Life* magazine on 9 November 1962,[19] and in 1992 he even invited 60 pioneers of bioethics to celebrate the 30th anniversary of the discipline. Marginalising and even ignoring Potter's incomparably richer and more complex ideas, Jonsen does not try to hide the direct and not very scientific pressure of the Kennedy Institute on Hellegers (and, in fact, does not see anything particularly problematic in it).[20]

There is the view that Potter was from the Midwest but that everything that is important in the USA takes place in the East, or that Potter was overshadowed by the very strong cult of Aldo Leopold, but this does not sound too convincing. (However, it is true that A. Leopold's son, the prominent plant physiologist Carl Leopold (1919-2009), tried to revive interest in his father's land ethic and casually referred to Potter in relation to it as 'one of many').[21] Of course, Potter's bioethics was, for Americans, deeper and more philosophised, and therefore less

---

[17] Renée C. Fox and Judith P. Swazey, *Observing Bioethics* (New York: Oxford University Press, 2008).

[18] Albert R. Jonsen, *The Birth of Bioethics* (New York: Oxford University Press, 1998), 27-34.

[19] Shana Alexander, 'They decide who lives, who dies', *Life* 53 (1962): 102-124.

[20] Albert R. Jonsen, 'The birth of bioethics: The origins and evolution of a demi-discipline', *Medical Humanities Review* 11, no. 1 (1997): 9-21.

[21] Cf. A. Carl Leopold, 'Living with the Land Ethic', *BioScience* 54, no. 2 (2004): 152 (149-154).

attractive than Georgetown principlism. However, it is almost certain that the direction of the development of bioethics was determined by the money and political influence of the Kennedy Institute and its favoured choices, who have appropriated bioethics and turned it into a lucrative global business. This policy of denying Potter's contribution seems to have become something of a plot and does not reflect well on American scientific historiography. (Or, as Potter's student Gerald Lower said: 'so much for the ethics of American ethicists'. Lower rightly points out Potter's global bioethics has mainly attracted Europeans rather than Americans.)[22] There are also those who ignore Potter out of honest ignorance. Of course, bioethics is certainly one of the most exciting areas today, but it is no wonder that in the ambitiously titled (and paid for) work *Bioethics in the 21st Century* not only is there no mention of Potter but in the flood of biomedical topics neither is mention made of any of the most significant authors.[23]

That this kind of thinking is not without foundation has been confirmed by one of the last of Potter's colleagues, Peter Whitehouse, who has twice had to cancel announced symposia (the first in Madison on Potter, and the second in Cleveland in 2015 on 'The ecological dimensions of bioethics').[24] Although it sounds strange, Whitehouse claims that both events had to be cancelled due to academic undermining.

A similar thing has happened in Anglophone literature with Jahr. In the recent book *Global Bioethics: What for?*, which was published in 2015 to mark the 20th anniversary of UNESCO's bioethics programme, of the 32 authors only Mary Rawlinson, Professor of Bioethics at Stony Brook University in New York, mentions Jahr and puts his work in context with Potter's. Potter is treated much better in the book, and is mentioned by as many as 6 authors. However, the contributions have been amusingly arranged by UNESCO, paying more attention to 'aesthetics' than relevance. There are 10 articles from Western Europe here, though there are not any from Germany, which is interesting. Eastern Europe is 'well covered' by a contribution from Slovakia and another from Belarus. There are four articles from Africa, one from Asia (from Thailand), and 8 from Latin America. Besides one article each from Canada and

---

22 Gerald M. Lower, 'Van Rensselaer Potter: A memoriam', *Cambridge Quarterly of Healthcare Ethics* 11 (2002): 329 (329-330).

23 Cf. Abraham Rudnick, ed., *Bioethics in the 21st Century* (Rijeka: InTech, 2011).

24 With just a small number of participants invited, the conference 'Ecological Dimensions of Bioethics: Plain Genealogy, Disciplinary Formation, and the Context of Health & Healthcare' should have been held at *Case Western Reserve* University in Cleveland, Ohio. The co-organisers, besides P. Whitehouse (who is Professor of Neurology at this university, as well as at the Baycrest Institute in Toronto), should have been Jeremy Bendik-Keymer, professor of ethics, and Jonathan Beever, post-doctoral fellow at Pennsylvania State University in Philadelphia.

Australia, there are three from the USA, which are, symbolically, the first and the last.[25] Just how arrogant the English-speaking world is when it comes to understanding modern trends in bioethics is also shown by the book *The Making of British Bioethics* by Duncan Wilson, who states that 'Potter's view of bioethics differs from the dictionary's definition, and designates an approach that is not familiar to us today '.[26]

Of course, it cannot be said that Potter did not have followers in the USA. Apart from the people in his Network, who were also connected to Potter personally, David Thomasma, for example, the editor of the *Cambridge Quarterly of Healthcare Ethics*, mentions that the first book on the shelf of the new Human Values and Health Studies Program of the University of Tennessee in Memphis was Potter's *Global Bioethics*, and that Potter's global outlook, as for many others, had shaped his career.[27] Since Thomasma began to fill his shelves in 1973 when the programme was established, that is, fifteen years before the publication of *Global Bioethics*, it seems likely that he was talking about Potter's first book, which was on bridge bioethics.

It is interesting to speculate on what would have happened if Potter and Callahan had combined their efforts. Their ideas were very similar (biomedical ethics, environmental ethics and population control), and their educations and horizons were broader (both of them read certain European authors) than those who from Georgetown dictated world trends in bioethics. Callahan had to experience similar frustrations to those of Potter, given how aggressively the Kennedy Institute occupied the bioethical space. Callahan was partly responsible for this development himself, insisting on independence from the university 'which was always imposing its policy' (which he had probably had the opportunity to see in the example of Georgetown). Was the mutual coldness of Potter and Callahan and their ignoring of each other caused by Callahan's Catholicism? Or were they doomed by their mutual contempt towards each other in the early 1970s? Perhaps feeling the potential of such an alliance, the Hastings Center invited Potter, as the author who had introduced the concept of bioethics, to comment on how the area had developed in an issue of the Center's journal in 1998.[28] However, this hand was extended a little too late, although the idea of bridging the 'ecomedical disconnection syndrome' (as Whitehouse called

[25] Germán Solinís, ed., *Global Bioethics: What for?* (Paris: UNESCO, 2015); http://unesdoc.unesco.org/images/0023/002311/231159e.pdf

[26] Duncan Wilson, *The Making of British Bioethics* (Manchester: Manchester University Press, 2014), 1.

[27] David C. Thomasma, 'Early bioethics', *Cambridge Quarterly of Helathcare Ethics* 11 (2002): 335 (335-343).

[28] Potter, 'Bioethics, biology, and the biosphere'.

it),[29] was in fact the right one. In any case, the synergy between Potter and Callahan would have changed the history of the discipline and better prepared the field in America for the ideas of Fritz Jahr.

The conflict between the logic of natural (and, of course, applied) science on the one hand, and social sciences and especially the humanities on the other, about which Potter spoke and wrote so much, is commonplace in our society. Has there not for years been controversy about the criteria imposed on scientists, philosophers and journals which are linked to academic advancement and support for projects, i.e. the existences of thousands of people?

In an alienated and globalised world blurred by the migration of people, goods and information, in which there are fewer people that we know or want to know (and the opinions of most of those we know we do not care about), the significance of ethics is being diminished. Even the laws in such a world are evaded, or exceptions are sought, or all intelligence is focused on avoiding sanctions – not because of social judgment, or so-called 'shame' (long ago, we understood the relativity of the laws being passed, as well as their choice of focus and the time of their application), but because of the material harm such sanctions can cause. In such a world that is quickly breaking down (or perhaps it has always been like this but we have only just awakened to the fact) and in which there is no renouncing of values but an inversion of their order on a scale of acceptability, it is difficult to think of ethics as something other than utopian or uchronic. Potter's pleas therefore take on a congenial sympathetic intellectual exercise like Cassandra's prophecies to the world regarding its not so great near future. For this reason, they will never lose their appeal.

[29] Cf. Peter J. Whitehouse, 'The ecomedical disconnection syndrome', *Hastings Center Report* 29, no. 1 (1999): 41-44.

LITERATURE

Akabayashi, Akira, editor. *The Future of Bioethics: International Dialogues*. Oxford: Oxford University Press, 2014.

Alexander, Shana. »They decide who lives, who dies«. *Life* 53 (1962): 102-124.

Baker, Robert. *Before Bioethics: A History of American Medical Ethics from the Colonial Period to the Bioethics Revolution*. New York: Oxford University Press, 2013.

Ballantyne, Andrew. *Arhitektura*. Preveo Mirzah Purić. Sarajevo: Šahinpašić, 2004.

Beauchamp, Tom L. »Does ethical theory have a future in bioethics?« *Journal of Law, Medicine, and Ethics* 32 (2004): 209-217.

Beauchamp, Tom L., and James F. Childress. *Principles of Biomedical Ethics*. 7th edition. New York/Oxford: Oxford University Press, 2013.

Belkin, Gary S. »Moving beyond bioethics: history and the search for medical humanism«. *Perspectives in Biology and Medicine* 47, no. 3 (2004): 374.

Bentham, Jeremy. *An Introduction to the Principles of Morals and Legislation*. Kitchener: Batoche Books, 1781/2000.

Boné, Édouard. »Les trois générations de la bioéthique«. *Revue théologique de Louvain* 24 (1993): 478-492.

Bracanović, Tomislav. »From integrative bioethics to pseudoscience«. *Developing World Bioethics* 12, no. 3 (2012): 148-156.

Brenner, Andreas. *Umweltethik: ein Lehr- und Lesebuch*. Würzburg: Königshausen & Neumann, 2014.

Brooks Pfeiffer, Bruce, editor. *The Essential Frank Lloyd Wright: Critical Writings on Architecture*. Princeton: Princeton University Press, 2008.

Brown, Harrison. *The Challenge of Man's Future*. New York: Viking Press, 1954.

Burris, R. H., C. A. Baumann and V. R. Potter. »Conrad Arnold Elvehjem, 1901-1962«. *Biographical Memoirs of the National Academy of Sciences* 59 (1990): 135-167.

Callahan, Daniel. »Bioethics«. In *Applied Ethics: Critical Concepts in Philosophy*. Edited by Ruth Chedwick and Doris Schroeder. London: Routledge, 2002, pp. 3-19.

Callahan, Daniel. *In Search of the Good: A Life in Bioethics*. Cambridge: MIT Press, 2012.

Callicott, J. Baird. »Animal liberation: a triangular affair«. *Environmental Ethics* 2 (1980): 311-338.

Callicott, J. Baird. »Environmental Ethics: I. overview«. In *Encyclopedia of Bioethics*. 3rd edition. Vol. 2. Edited by Stephen Post. New York: Macmillan Reference USA, 2004, pp. 757-769.

Carson, Rachel. *Silent Spring*. Boston/London: Houghton Mifflin/Penguin Books, 1962/2000.

Carstensen, Vernon. »A century of Land-Grant colleges«. *The Journal of Higher Education* 33, no. 1 (1962): 30-37.

Carstensen, Vernon. »The origin and early development of the Wisconsin Idea«. *Wisconsin Magazine of History* 39, no. 3 (1956): 181-188.

Chiarelli, Brunetto. »Global Bioethics: a suggested distinction between ethic and morality«. In *Implementing Ecological Integrity: Restoring Regional and Global Environmental and Human Health*. Edited by P. Crabbé, A. J. Holland, L. Ryszkowski and L. Westra. Dordrecht: Springer, 2000, pp. 351-360.

Chiarelli, Brunetto. »Man, nature and ethics: Global Bioethics«. *Global Bioethics* 5, no. 1 (1992): 13-20.

Chiarelli, Brunetto. »The bioecologica bases of Global Bioethics«. *Global Bioethics* 25, no. 1 (2014): 19-26.

Chiarelli, Brunetto. *Bioetica globale*. Firenze: Angelo Pontecorboli, 1993.

Clements, Colleen D. »'Therefore choose life': reconciling medical and environmental bioethics«. *Perspectives in Biology and Medicine* 28, no. 3 (1985): 407-425.

Crisp, Roger, editor. *The Oxford Handbook of the History of Ethics*. Oxford: Oxford University Press, 2013.

Čović, Ante. »Integrativna bioetika i pluriperspektivizam«. In *Integrativna bioetika i izazovi suvremene civilizacije*. Edited by Velimir Valjan. Sarajevo: Bioeticko drustvo u BiH, 2007, pp. 65-75.

D'Alisa, Giacomo, Federico Demaria and Giorgos Kallis, editors. *Degrowth: A Vocabulary For a New Era*. New York/London: Routledge, 2015.

Daniels, Jessica M. »In ethics professionals need education«. *The Record*, January 31, 1974.

Dell'Oro, Roberto. »Oltre la censura del senso: riflessioni sul futuro della bioetica«. *Medicina e morale* 63, no. 2 (2014): 233-246.

Devall, Bill, and George Sessions, editors. *Deep Ecology: Living as if Nature Mattered*. Salt Lake City/Layton: Gibbs M. Smith, Inc./Peregrine Smith Books, 1985.

Dobzhansky, Theodosius. »Nothing in biology makes sense except in the light of evolution«. *American Biology Teacher* 35 (1973): 125-129.

Dobzhansky, Theodosius. «Evolution at work». *Science* 127, no. 3306 (1958): 1091-1098.

Dobzhansky, Theodosius. *Genetics and the Origin of Species*. New York: Columbia University Press, 1937.

Doris, Margaret E. »Land-Grant Ideology, the Wisconsin Idea, and the Foundations of Van Rensselaer Potter's Bioethics«. PhD Thesis. Faculty of Theology – Boston University, 2014.

Doris, Margaret. »Land-Grant ideology, the Wisconsin Idea, and the foundations of Van Rensselaer Potter's bioethics«. In *American Society for Bioethics + Humanities, Annual Meeting, October 24-27, 2013, Atlanta, GA*. Atlanta: ASBH, 2013, p. 43.

Ehrlich, Paul R. *The Population Bomb*. New York: Ballantine Books, 1968/1970.

Emerson, Ralph Waldo. *Essays*. New York: Harper Colophon Books, 1926/1951.

Engelhardt, H. Tristram Jr. »The recent history of Christian bioethics critically reassesed«. *Christian Bioethics* 20, no. 2 (2014): 146-167.

Engelhardt, H. Tristram Jr. *The Foundations of Bioethics*. New York/Oxford: Oxford University Press, 1986.

Engelhardt, H. Tristram. »Introduction: bioethics as a global phenomenon«. In *The Annals of Bioethics: Regional Perspectives in Bioethics*. Edited by J. F. Peppin and M. J. Cherry. London/New York: Taylor and Francis, 2008, pp. xiii-xxii.

Evans, John H. *The History and Future of Bioethics: A Sociological View*. New York: Oxford University Press, 2012.

Favraux, Paul, and Albert Chapelle. »Bioéthique et foi chrétienne: à propos d'un livre récent«. *Nouvelle revue théologique* 108 (1986): 249-267.

Fox Michael W. *Inhumane Society: The American Way of Exploiting Animals*. New York: St. Martin's Press, 1990.

Fox, Michael W. *Beyond Evolution: The Genetically Altered Future of Plants, Animals, the Earth... and Humans*. New York: The Lyons Press, 1999.

Fox, Michael W. *Bringing Life to Ethics: Global Bioethics for a Humane Society*. Albany: State University of New York Press, 2001.

Fox, Renée C., and Judith P. Swazey. *Observing Bioethics*. New York: Oxford University Press, 2008.

Franke, Kurt W., and Van R. Potter. »A new toxicant occuring naturally in certain samples of plant foodstuffs«. *The Journal of Nutrition* 8, no. 6 (1934): 615-624.

Franke, Kurt W., and Van R. Potter. »The effect of selenium containing foodstuffs on growth and reproduction of rats at various ages«. *The Journal of Nutrition* 12, no. 2 (1936): 205-214.

Franke, Kurt W., and Van Rensselaer Potter. »The ability of rats to discriminate between diets of varying degrees of toxicity«. *Science* 83, no. 2153 (1936): 330-332.

Friedman Ross, Lainie. »Forty years later: the scope of bioethics revisited«. *Perspectives in Biology and Medicine* 53, no. 3 (2010): 452-457.

Gensabella, Marianna. »Biodiversity and the Global Bioethics of Van Rensselaer Potter«. In *Proceedings of the 1st EMUNI Research Souk 2009 (EMUNI ReS 2009): The Euro-Mediterranean Student Research Multi-Conference*. Messina: Università degli Studi di Messina, 2009, pp. 1-13.

Gensabella Furnari, Marianna. »The scientist demanding wisdom: the 'Bridge to the Future' by Van Rensselaer Potter«. *Perspectives in Biology and Medicine* 45, no. 1 (2002): 31-42.

Gilligan, Carol. *In a Different Voice: Psychological Theory and Women's Development*. Cambridge, MA/London: Harvard University Press, 1982.

Gould, Whitney. »Bio-ethics« creed emerges from »E-Week« observance as a new type of religion«. *Madison Capital Times*, April 25, 1970.

Gregory, Michael S. »Science and humanities: toward a new worldview«. In *The Culture of Biomedicine, Studies in Science and Culture*. Vol. 1. Edited by Heyward Brock and Ann Harward. Newark/London/Toronto: University of Delaware Press/Associated University Press, 1984, pp. 11-33.

Gribble, Roger. »Auditorium unit of 12 confirmed«. *Wisconsin State Journal*, June 25, 1965.

Gruen, Lori, and William Ruddick. »Biomedical and environmental ethics alliance: common causes and grounds«. *Bioethical Inquiry* 6 (2009): 457-466.

Gustafson, James M. »Response to Van Rensselaer Potter, 'Getting to the year 3000: can Global Bioethics overcome evolution's fatal flaw?« *Perspectives in Biology and Medicine* 35, no. 3 (1992): 339-344.

Hare, F. Kenneth. »How should we treat environment: university organization presently permits only piecemeal consideration of environmental problems«. *Science* 167, no. 3917 (1970): 352-355.

Henley, Jon. »The forgotten Kennedy«. *The Guardian*, August 13, 2009.

Hoeveler, J. David. »The university and the Social Gospel: the intellectual origins of the Wisconsin Idea«. *Wisconsin Magazine of History* 59, no. 4 (1976): 282-298.

Holm, Søren, and Bryn Williams-Jones. »Global bioethics – myth or reality?« *BMC Medical Ethics* 7, no. 10 (2006): 1-10.

Irving, Dianne N. »The bioethics mess«. *Crisis Magazine* 19, no. 5 (2001).

Iseminger, Jeff. »Potter prescribes 'Global Bioethics' in Leopold tradition«. *Wisconsin State Journal*, February 26, 1989.

Iseminger, Jeff. »R: Bioethics – brightening our lives«. *Wisconsin Week*, February 22, 1989.

Jahr, Fritz. »Bio-Ethik: eine Umschau über die ethischen Beziehungen des Menschen zu Tier und Pflanze«. *Kosmos* 24, no. 1 (1927): 2-4.

Jahr, Fritz. »Gesinnungsdiktatur oder Gedankenfreiheit? Gedanken über eine liberale Gestaltung des Gesinnungunterrichts«. *Die neue Erziehung* 12 (1930): 200-202.

Jahr, Fritz. »Wege zum sexualen Ethos«. *Ethik: Sexual- und Gesellschaftsethik* 4, no. 10-11 (1928): 161-163.

Jameton, Andrew. »Global Bioethics«. *Cambridge Quarterly of Helathcare Ethics* 3, no. 3 (1994): 449-466.

Jennings, Bruce. »Beyond the social contract of consumption: democratic governance in the post-carbon era«. *Critical Policy Studies* 4, no. 3 (2010): 222-233.

Jennings, Bruce. »Putting the bios back into bioethics: prospects for health and climate justice«. In *Climate Change and Health: Bioethical Insights into Values and Policy*. Edited by Cheryl Cox Macpherson. Springer USA, 2015, pp. 1-39.

Jennings, Bruce. »Toward an ecological political economy: accommodating nature in a new discourse of public philosophy and policy analysis«. *Critical Policy Studies* 4, no. 1 (2010): 77-85.

Jonsen, Albert R. »The birth of bioethics: the origins and evolution of a demi-discipline«. *Medical Humanities Review* 11, no. 1 (1997): 9-21.

Jonsen, Albert R. »Why has bioethics become so boring?« *Journal of Medical Philosophy* 25, no. 6 (2000): 689-699

Jonsen, Albert R. *The Birth of Bioethics*. New York: Oxford University Press, 1998.

Jurić, Hrvoje. »Uporišta za integrativnu bioetiku u djelu Van Rensselaera Pottera«. In *Integrativna bioetika i izazovi suvremene civilizacije: zbornik radova Prvog međunarodnog bioetičkog simpozija u Bosni i Hercegovini*

(Sarajevo, 31. III.-1. IV. 2006.). Edited by Velimir Valjan. Sarajevo: Bioetičko društvo u BiH, 2007, pp. 77-99.

Kaebnick, Gregory E. *Humans in Nature: The World as We Find It and the World as We Create It*. Oxford/New York: Oxford University Press, 2014.

Kieffer, George H. *Bioethics: A Textbook of Issues*. Reading: Addison-Wesley Publishing Co., 1979.

Kukoč, Mislav. »Introduction: philosophy and globalization I«. *Synthesis philosophica* 47, no. 1 (2009), 3-5.

Küng, Hans. *Global Responsibility: A Search for a New World Ethic*. New York: Continuum Publishing Co., 1993.

Leopold, A. Carl. »Living with the Land Ethic«. *BioScience* 54, no. 2 (2004): 149-154.

Leopold, Aldo. *A Sand County Almanac*. New York. Ballantine Books, 1949/1970.

Lloyd Wright, Frank. »Organic architecture«. In *Truth Against the World*. Edited by Patrick J. Meehan. Washington, D.C.: The Preservation Press & National Trust for Historic Preservation, 1992.

Loew, Patty. *Seventh Generation Earth Ethics: Native Voices of Wisconsin*. Madison: Wisconsin Historical Society Press, 2014.

Lower, Gerald M. »Van Rensselaer Potter: a memoriam«. *Cambridge Quarterly of Healthcare Ethics* 11 (2002): 329-330.

Marty, Martin E., and Dean A. Peerman, editors. *New Theology: No. 10*. New York: Collier Macmillan, 1973.

McLuhan, M. *The Gutenberg Galaxy: The Making of Typographic Man*. Toronto: University of Toronto Press, 1962.

Mead, Margaret. »Towards more vivid utopias«. *Science* 126, no. 3280 (1957): 957-961.

Mead, Margaret. *Continuities in Cultural Evolution*. New Haven, CT: Yale University Press, 1964.

Meine, Curt. »Aldo Leopold: connecting conservation science, ethics, policy, and practice«. In *Linking Ecology and Ethics for a Changing World: Values, Philosophy, and Action*. Edited by R. Rozzi, S. T. A. Pickett, C. Palmer, J. J. Arnesto and J. B. Callicott. Dordrecht: Springer, 2013, pp. 173-184.

Meine, Curt. »Biodiversity conservation«. In *Bioethics* (*Encyclopedia of Bioethics*). 4th edition. Edited by Bruce Jennings. Farmington Hills: Macmillan Reference USA, 2014.

Meine, Curt. »Leopold, Aldo (1887-1949)« (sic!). In *Encyclopedia of Religion and Nature*. Edited by Bron Taylor. London/New York: Continuum, 2005, pp. 1005-1008.

Meine, Curt. »Van Renssalaer Potter: Global Bioethics: Building on the Leopold Legacy«. *Environmental Ethics* 11, no. 3 (1989): 281-285.

Meine, Curt. *Aldo Leopold: His Life and Work*. Madison: University of Wisconsin Press, 1988.

Merlo, Paolo. »Introduzione storica alla bioetica«. In *Dalla parte della vita – I: Itinerari di bioetica – I*. Edited by Giuseppe Zeppegno and Enrico Laghero. Cantalupa: Effatà Editrice, 2007, pp. 11-33.

Milbrath, Lester W. *Learning to Think Environmentally While There is Still Time*. Albany: State University of New York Press, 1996.

Milstead, William W. »Review: Bioethics – Bridge to the Future by Van Rensselaer Potter«. *American Biology Teacher* 33, no. 9 (1971): 560-561.

Morandini, Simone. *Teologija i ekologija*. Translated by Slavko Antunović. Zagreb: Kršćanska sadašnjost, 2013.

Mori, Maurizio. »Bioethics in Italy up to 2002: an overview«. In *Bioethics and Moral Content: National Traditions of Health Care Morality*. Edited by H. Tristram Engelhardt and Lisa M. Rasmussen. Dordrecht/Boston/London: Kluwer Academic Publishers, 2002, pp. 97-120.

Mumford, Lewis. *The Story of Utopias*. New York: Viking Press, 1922/1962.

Muzur, Amir, and Hans-Martin Sass, editors. *Fritz Jahr and the Foundations of Global Bioethics: The Future of Integrative Bioethics*. Münster: Lit, 2012.

Muzur, Amir, and Iva Rinčić. »Two kinds of globality: a comparison of Fritz Jahr and Van Rensselaer Potter's bioethics«. *Global Bioethics* 26, no. 1 (2015): 23-27.

N. N. »Cancer pioneer Potter dies«. *The Capital Times*, September 11, 2001.

N. N. »Know your Madisonian: Van R. Potter«. *Wisconsin State Journal*, December 19, 1972.

N. N. »Man into superman: the promise and peril of the new genetics«. *Time*, Aptil 19, 1971, 33-52.

N. N. »New beachhead in war on cancer reached, U. W.'s Dr. Potter reports«. *Wisconsin State Journal*, September 17, 1947.

N. N., Pierpoint Centennial: 1887-1987. Pierpont: Langford Bugle, 1987.

N. N. »Professor of oncology Van R. Potter retires«. *Wisconsin Medical Alumni Quarterly* 22, no. 3 (1982): 17.

Næss, Arne. »The deep ecological movement: some philosophical aspects«. In *Deep Ecology for the 21st Century: Readings on the Philosophy and Practice of the New Environmentalism*. Edited by George Sessions. Boston/London: Shambala, 1995, pp. 64-84.

Neutra, Richard J. *Survival through Design*. New York: Oxford University Press, 1954.

Pascual, Fernando. »Alcune riflessioni sulla 'bioetica' di Potter«. *Alpha Omega* 5 (2002): 309-336.

Pierce, Jessica, and George Randels. *Contemporary Bioethics: A Reader with Cases*. New York: Oxford University Press, 2010.

Platt, John R. »What we must do«. *Science* 166 (1969): 1115-1121.

Platt, John R. *The Step to Man*. New York: Wiley, 1966.

Platt, John R., editor. *New Views on the Nature of Man*. Chicago: Chicago University Press, 1965.

Pollard, Irina. *Bioscience Ethics*. New York: Cambridge University Press, 2009.

Potter, Robert Lyman. »From clinical ethics to prganizational ethics: the second stage of the evolution of bioethics«. *Bioethics Forum* (1996): 3-12.

Potter, V. R., D. A. Baerreis, R. A. Bryson, J. W. Curvin, G. Johansen, J. McLeod, J. Rankin and K. R. Symon. »Purpose and function of the university«. *Science* 167, no. 3925 (1970): 1590-1593.

Potter, Van Rensselaer, and Conrad A. Elvehjem. »A modified method for the study of tissue oxidations«. *Journal of Biological Chemistry* 114, no. 2 (1936): 495-504.

Potter, Van Rensselaer, and Peter J. Whitehouse. »Deep and Global Bioethics for a livable Third Millennium«. *The Scientist* 12 (1998): 1-9.

Potter, Van Rensselaer, and Richard Grantham. »Scientists' responsibility for survival of the human species«. *The Scientist* 6, no. 11 (1992): 10-11.

Potter, Van Rensselaer, editor. *Methods in Medical Research.* Vol. 1. Chicago: Year Book Publishers, 1948.

Potter, Van Rensselaer. »Biocybernetics and survival«. *Zygon* 5, no. 3 (1970): 229-246.

Potter, Van Rensselaer. »Bioethics and the human prospect: the meaning of survival«. *Wisconsin Medical Alumni Quarterly* 23, no. 4 (1983): 19.

Potter, Van Rensselaer. »Bioethics: the science of survival«. *Perspectives in Biology and Medicine* 14 (1970): 127-153.

Potter, Van Rensselaer. »Blocked ontogeny«. *Science* 28 (1987): 964.

Potter, Van Rensselaer. »Disorder as a built in component of biological systems: the survival imperative«. *Zygon* 6, no. 2 (1971): 135-150.

Potter, Van Rensselaer. »How is an optimum environment defined?« *Environmental Research* 2, no. 5 (1969): 476-487.

Potter, Van Rensselaer. »Intracellular responses to environmental change: the quest for optimum environment«. *Environmental Research* 3, no. 2 (1970): 176-186.

Potter, Van Rensselaer. »On the road to the blocked ontogeny theory«. *Advances in Oncology* 4, no. 1 (1988): 3-8.

Potter, Van Rensselaer. »Phenotypic diversity in experimental hepatomas: the concept of partially blocked ontogeny«. *British Journal of Cancer* 38, no. 1 (1978): 1-23.

Potter, Van Rensselaer. »Society and science: can science aid in the search for sophistication in dealing with order and disorder in human affairs?« *Science* 146, no. 3647 (1964): 1018-1022.

Potter, Van Rensselaer. »The present status of the blocked ontogeny hypothesis of neoplasia: the thalassemia connection«. *Oncodevelopmental Biology and Medicine* 2 (1981): 243-266.

Potter, Van Rensselaer. »A new protocol and its rationale for the study of initiation and promotion of carcinogenesis in rat liver«. *Carcinogenesis* 2, no. 12 (1981): 1375-1379.

Potter, Van Rensselaer. »A plea for formal support for study and reflection«. *Cancer Research* 16, no. 8 (1956): 725-727.

Potter, Van Rensselaer. »A response to Clements: environmental bioethics – a call for controlled human fertility in a healthy ecosystem«. *Perspectives in Biology and Medicine* 28, no. 3 (1985): 426–433.

Potter, Van Rensselaer. »Bioethics and the human prospect«. In *The Culture of Biomedicine. Studies in Science and Culture*. Vol. 1. Edited by Heyward Brock and Ann Harward. Newark/London/Toronto: University of Delaware Press/Associated University Press, 1984, pp. 124-137.

Potter, Van Rensselaer. »Bioethics for whom?« *Annals of the New York Academy of Sciences* 196 (1972): 200–205.

Potter, Van Rensselaer. »Bioethics looks at survival with a long view«. *Madison Capital Times*, April 9, 1979.

Potter, Van Rensselaer. »Bioethics: state-of-the-art books«. *BioScience* 31, no. 2 (1981): 172.

Potter, Van Rensselaer. »Bridge to the future: the concept of human progress«. *Land Economics* 38, no. 1 (1962): 1-8.

Potter, Van Rensselaer. »Cancer: the known and the unknown«. *Wisconsin State Journal*, February 13 and 15, 1951.

Potter, Van Rensselaer. »Council on the future«. *Nation*, February 8, 1965.

Potter, Van Rensselaer. »Emeritus Professors can, Assistant Professors mustn't«. *The FASEB Journal* 7 (1993): 255-256.

Potter, Van Rensselaer. »Bioethics, biology, and the biosphere: fragmented ethics and 'Bridge Bioethics'«. *Hastings Center Report* 29, no. 1 (1999): 38-40.

Potter, Van Rensselaer. »Getting to the Year 3000: can Global Bioethics overcome evolution's fatal flaw?« *Perspectives in Biology and Medicine* 34 (1990): 89-98.

Potter, Van Rensselaer. »Global Bioethics as a secular source of moral authority for long-term human survival«. *Global Bioethics* 5, no. 1 (1992): 5-11.

Potter, Van Rensselaer. »Global Bioethics facing a world in crisis«. *Global Bioethics* 5, no. 1 (1992): 69-76.

Potter, Van Rensselaer. »Global Bioethics: linking genes to ethical behavior«. *Perspectives in Biology and Medicine* 39, no. 1 (1995): 118-131.

Potter, Van Rensselaer. »Global Bioethics: origin and development«. In *Handbook for Environmental Risk Decision Making: Values, Perceptions, and Ethics*. Edited by C. Richard Cothern. Boca Raton: CRC Lewis Publishers, 1996, pp. 359-373.

Potter, Van Rensselaer. »Humility with responsibility – a bioethic for oncologists«. *Cancer Research* 35 (1975): 2297-2306.

Potter, Van Rensselaer. »Initiation and promotion in cancer formation: the importance of studies on intracellular communication«. *The Yale Journal of Biology and Medicine* 53 (1980): 367-384.

Potter, Van Rensselaer. »Introduction: evolving ethical concepts«. *BioScience* 27, no. 4 (1977): 251-253.

Potter, Van Rensselaer. »Moving the culture toward more vivid utopias with survival as the goal«. *Global Bioethics* 14, no. 4 (2001): 19-30.

Potter, Van Rensselaer. »New horizons in cancer research«. *Wisconsin Cancer Bulletin* 20, no. 3 (1958): 5-10.

Potter, Van Rensselaer. »On dying with personhood: Socratic death«. *Perspectives in Biology and Medicine* 43, no. 1 (1999): 103-111.

Potter, Van Rensselaer. »Physiological adaptation at the molecular level: the frontier where research on differentiation and malignancy meet«. *Perspectives in Biology and Medicine* 24, no. 4 (1981): 525-542.

Potter, Van Rensselaer. »Probabilistic aspects of the human cybernetic machine«. *Perspectives in Biology and Medicine* 17, no. 2 (1974): 164-183.

Potter, Van Rensselaer. »Professor: bioethics institutes vital today«. *Wisconsin State Journal*, December 1, 1991.

Potter, Van Rensselaer. »Real Bioethics: biocentric or anthropocentric?« *Ethics and the Environment* 1, no. 2 (1996): 177-183.

Potter, Van Rensselaer. »Recent trends in cancer biochemistry: the importance of studies on fetal tissue«. *Proceedings: Canadian Cancer Conference* 8 (1969): 9-30.

Potter, Van Rensselaer. »Science, religion must share quest for global survival«. *The Scientist*, May 16, 1994.

Potter, Van Rensselaer. »Studies on enzyme inhibition – 50 years ago«. *The FASEB Journal* 7 (1993): 486-487.

Potter, Van Rensselaer. »Teilhard de Chardin and the concept of purpose«. *Zygon* 3, no. 4 (1968): 367-376.

Potter, Van Rensselaer. »The cancer analogy«. In *Learning to Listen to the Land*. Edited by Bill Willers. Washington: Island Press, 1991, pp. 157-162.

Potter, Van Rensselaer. »The ethics of nature and nurture«. *Zygon* 8, no. 1 (1973): 36-47.

Potter, Van Rensselaer. »The genetic aspects of the enzyme-virus theory of cancer«. *Science* 101, no. 2633 (1945): 609-610.

Potter, Van Rensselaer. »The homogenate technique«. *Methods in Medical Research* 1 (1948): 317-336.

Potter, Van Rensselaer. »The intellectual ‚last will' of the first global bioethicist«. In *Fritz Jahr and the Foundations of Global Bioethics: the Future of Integrative Bioethics*. Edited by Amir Muzur and Hans-Martin Sass. Münster: Lit, 2012, pp. 149-157.

Potter, Van Rensselaer. »The role of nutrition in cancer prevention«. *Science* 101, no. 2614 (1945): 105-109.

Potter, Van Rensselaer. »The role of the individual in modern society«. In *Changing Concepts of Productive Living*. Edited by Robert Dean Boyd. Madison: University of Wisconsin – University Extension, 1967, pp. 37-51.

Potter, Van Rensselaer. »What does bioethics mean?« *The Ag Bioethics Forum* 8, no. 1 (1996); (http://www.bioethics.iastate.edu/forum/jun.96pg2.html).

Potter, Van Rensselaer. »Years with Conrad Elvehjem«. In *One Hundred Years of Agricultural Chemistry and Biochemistry at Wisconsin: A Steenbock Symposium*. Edited by David L. Nelson and Brook Chase Soltvedt. Madison: Science Tech Publishers, 1989.

Potter, Van Rensselaer. »Years with Elizabeth and James Miller: in appreciation«. In *Biological Reactive Intermediates 111*. Edited by James J. Kocsis, David J. Jollow, Charlotte M. Witmer, Judd O. Nelsen and Robert Snyder. New York: Plenum Publishing Corporation, 1986.

Potter, Van Rensselaer. *Bioethics: Bridge to the Future*. Englewood Cliffs: Prentice-Hall, Inc., 1971.

Potter, Van Rensselaer. *Bioetika: most prema budućnosti*. Translated by Ines Radinović. Rijeka: Katedra za društvene znanosti Medicinskog fakulteta u Rijeci/Hrvatsko društvo za kliničku bioetiku/Hrvatsko bioetičko društvo/Međunarodno udruženje za kliničku bioetiku, 2007.

Potter, Van Rensselaer. *DNA Model Kit for Preparing – Dimensional Models of the Deoxyribonucleic Acid Double Helix According to the Watson-Crick Theory*. Minneapolis: Burgess Publishing Co., 1959.

Potter, Van Rensselaer. *Global Bioethics: Building on the Leopold Legacy*. East Lansing: Michigan State University Press, 1988.

Rayl, A. J. S. »Emeritus status offers some distinguished faculty a chance to parlay investigations on higher level«. *The Scientist*, November 9, 1992.

Reich, Warren T. »How bioethics got its name«. *The Hastings Center Report* 23, Suppl. 6 (1993): S6-S7.

Reich, Warren Thomas. »Revisiting the launching of the Kennedy Institute: re-visioning the origins of bioethics«. *Kennedy Institute of Ethics Journal* 6, no. 4 (1996): 323-327.

Reich, Warren Thomas. »The 'wider view': André Hellegers' passionate, integrating intellect and the creation of bioethics«. *Kennedy Institute of Ethics Journal* 9, no. 1 (1999): 25-51.

Reich, Warren Thomas. »The word 'bioethics': its birth and the legacies who shaped it«. *Kennedy Institute of Ethics Journal* 4, no. 4 (1994): 319-335.

Reich, Warren Thomas. »The word 'bioethics': the struggle over its earliest meanings«. *Kennedy Institute of Ethics Journal* 5, no. 1 (1995): 19-34.

Rensberger, Boyce. »Scientists seek a watchdog plan; system would alert public to dangers in laboratories«. *New York Times*, December 19, 1971.

Rinčić, Iva, and Amir Muzur. »Fritz Jahr: the invention of bioethics and beyond«. *Perspectives in Biology and Medicine* 54, no. 4 (2011): 550-556.

Rinčić, Iva, and Amir Muzur. »Od bioetičara-učenika do bioetičara-učitelja: pijetizam i edukacija u životu i djelu Fritza Jahra«. *Jahr* 3, no. 5 (2012): 111-116.

Rinčić, Iva, and Amir Muzur. »Variety of bioethics in Croatia: a historical sketch and a critical touch«. *Synthesis Philosophica* 26, no. 2 (2011): 403-428.

Rinčić, Iva, and Amir Muzur. *Fritz Jahr i rađanje europske bioetike*. Zagreb: Pergamena, 2012.

Risjord, Norman K. *Wisconsin: The Story of the Badger State*. Madison: Wisconsin Tails & Trials, 1995.

Rudnick, Abraham, editor. *Bioethics in the 21st Century*. Rijeka: InTech, 2011.

Rusch, Harold P. *Something Attempted, Something Done: A Personal History of Cancer Research at the University of Wisconsin, 1934-1979*. Madison: Wisconsin Medical Alumni Association, 1984.

Russo, Giovanni. »Storia della bioetica dalle origini ad oggi«. In *Storia della bioetica: le origini, il significato, le istituzioni*. Edited by Giovanni Russo. Roma: Armando Editore, 1995, pp. 7-99.

Russo, Giovanni. »Un rapporto sulla bioetica dai pionieri«. In *Bilancio di venticinque anni di bioetica*. Edited by Giovanni Russo. Torino: Editrice Elle, 1997, pp. 5-24.

Ryan, Rebecca. »Rebranding basic«. *Madison Magazine*, October 2014, 70-85.

Sacchi, Cesare F. »Il Gruppo 'G. Gadio' per l'Ecologia di base: origini e motivi«. *Studi Trentini di Scienze Naturali – Acta Biologica* 78, no. 1 (2001): 13-17.

Sakamoto, Hyakudai. »Towards a new 'Global Bioethics'«. *Bioethics* 13, no. 3-4 (1999): 191-197.

Sass, Hans-Martin, editor. *Bioethik in den USA: Methoden, Themen, Positionen*. Berlin/Heidelberg/New York/London/Paris/Tokyo: Springer-Verlag, 1988.

Sass, Hans-Martin, and Zhai Xiaomei. »Global Bioethics: Eastern or Western principles?« *Asian Bioethics Review* 3, no. 1 (2011): 1-2.

Scholte, J. A. *What is Globalization? The Definitional Issue – Again*. Coventry: Department of Politics and International Studies, University of Warwick, 2002.

Schott, T. »The world scientific community: globality and globalisation«. *Minerva* 29, no. 4 (1991): 440-461.

Schuler, Michael A. *Making the Good Life Last: Four Keys to Sustainable Living*. San Francisco: Berrett-Koehler Publishers, Inc., 2009.

Schweitzer, Albert. *An Anthology*. Translated by Charles R. Joy. Boston: Beacon, 1947.

Sessions, George. »1984: a postscript«. In *Deep Ecology: Living as if Nature Mattered*. Edited by Bill Devall and George Sessions. Salt Lake City/Layton: Gibbs M. Smith, Inc./Peregrine Smith Books, 1985, pp. 254-256.

Sessions, George. »Ecocentrism and the anthropocentric detour«. In *Deep Ecology for the 21st Century: Readings on the Philosophy and Practice of the New Environmentalism*. Edited by George Sessions. Boston/London: Shambala, 1995, pp. 156-183.

Solinís, Germán, editor. *Global Bioethics: What for?* Pariz: UNESCO, 2015.

Soros, George. »Toward a global open society«. *The Atlantic Monthly*, January 1998, 20-32.

Spagnolo, Antonio G. »L'imperativo bioetico«. *Medicina e morale* 1 (2010): 9-14.

Speybroeck, Linda van. »From epigenesis to epigentics: the case of C. H. Waddington«. *Annual of the New York Academy of Sciences* 981 (2002): 61-81.

Spinsanti, Sandro. *La bioetica: biografie per una disciplina*. Milano: Franco Angeli, 1995.

Stevens, M. L. Tina. *Bioethics in America: Origins and Cultural Politics*. Baltimore/London: The Johns Hopkins University Press, 2000.

Stossel, Scott. *Sarge: The Life and Times of Sargent Shriver*. Washington: Smithsonian Books, 2004.

Sulmasy, Daniel P. »In defense of the Amphibians: a critical appraisal of Engelhardt on the recent history of Christian bioethics«. *Christian Bioethics* 20, no. 2 (2014): 187-195.

Šegota, Ivan. »Intervjui: Van Rensselaer Potter, Rihito Kimura, Albert Jonsen, Hyakudai Sakamoto«. *Bioetički svesci* 19 (1999).

Taylor, Paul W. *Respect for Nature: A Theory of Environmental Ethics*. Princeton: Princeton University Press, 1986.

Teale, Edwin Way, editor. *The Wilderness World of John Muir*. Boston/New York: Mariner Books, 1954/2001.

Teilhard de Chardin, Pierre. *The Future of Man*. Translated by Norman Denny. London/New York: Wm. Collins Sons & Co., Ltd./Harper & Row, Publishers, 1964.

Teilhard de Chardin, Pierre. *The Phenomenon of Man*. Translated by Bernard Wall. London/New York: Wm. Collins Sons & Co., Ltd./Harper & Brothers, 1959.

ten Have, Henk A. M. J. »Potter's notion of bioethics«. *Kennedy Institute of Ethics Journal* 22, no. 1 (2012): 59-82.

ten Have, Henk. »Global Bioethics and communitarianism«. *Theoretical Medicine and Bioethics* 32, no. 5 (2011): 315-326.

Thomasma, David C. »Early bioethics«. *Cambridge Quarterly of Helathcare Ethics* 11 (2002): 335-343.

Torchio, Menico. »Venti anni di bioetica naturalistica in Italia (1973-1993)«. In *La vita e l'uomo nell'etàdelle teconolgie riptoduttive: una domanda di sapienza e di agire responsabile*. Edited by Elio Sgreccia and Marinella Lombardi Ricci. Milano: Università Cattolica del Sacro Cuore, 1997, pp. 3-6.

Trosko James E., and Henry C. Pitot. »In memoriam: Professor Emeritus Van Rensselaer Potter II (1911-2001)«. *Cancer Research* 63 (2003): 1724.

Trosko, James E. »Scientific concepts of human nature and their implications to bioethics in a Scientific and Technoligically-Altered World«. *Journal of the International Society of Bioethics* (SIBI) 9 (2003): 68-83.

Trosko, James E. »Scientific views of human nature: implications for the ethics of technological intervention«. In *The Culture of Biomedicine, Studies in Science and Culture*. Vol. 1. Edited by Heyward Brock and Ann Harward. Newark/London/Toronto: University of Delaware Press/Associated University Press, 1984, pp. 70-97.

Vukelich, George. »Bioethics and macho morality«. *Isthmus*, July 14, 1989.

Waddington, C. H. »The epigenotype«. *Endeavour*, January 1942, 18-20

Waddington, Conrad H. *The Ethical Animal*. Chicago: University of Chicago Press, 1967.

Wallace, Anthony F. C. *Religious Revitalization: A Function of Religion in Human History and Evolution.* Boston: Institute on Religion in an Age of Science, 1962.

Walter, Jennifer K., and Eran P. Klein, editors. *The Story of Bioethics: From Seminal Works to Contemporary Explorations*. Washington: Georgetown University Press, 2003.

Weber, Andreas. *Sve osjeća: čovjek, priroda i revolucija prirodnih znanosti*. Translated by Boris Perić. Zagreb: Naklada Ljevak, 2011.

Westra, Laura S. »The principle of 'Integrity' and *The Economy of the Earth*«. *Global Bioethics* 5, no. 1 (1992): 21-30.

White, Lynn. »The historical roots of our ecological crisis«. *Science* 155, no. 3767 (1967): 1203-1207.

Whitehouse, Peter J. »The ecomedical disconnection syndrome«. *Hastings Center Report* 29, no. 1 (1999): 41-44.

Whitehouse, Peter J. »The rebirth of bioethics: a tribute to Van Rensselaer Potter«. *Global Bioethics* 14, no. 4 (2001): 39.

Whitehouse, Peter J. »The rebirth of bioethics: extending the original formulations of Van Rensselaer Potter«. *American Journal of Bioethics* 3, no. 4 (2003): W26-W31.

Whitehouse, Peter J. »Van Rensselaer Potter: an intellectual memoir«. *Cambridge Quarterly of Healthcare Ethics* 11 (2002): 331-334.

Whitehouse, Peter. »Toward a deeper bioethics«. *Minding Nature* 3, no. 3 (2010): 18-24.

Wilches Flórez, Ángela Maria. »La propuesta bioética de Van Rensselaer Potter, cuatro décadas después«. *Opción* 27, no. 66 (2011): 70-84.

Williams, Erin D. »A legacy of bioethical sustainability: in memory of Dr. Van Rensselaer Potter II«. *Global Bioethics* 14, no. 4 (2001): 49-58.

Wilson, Duncan. *The Making of British Bioethics*. Manchester: Manchester University Press, 2014.

Wineke, William R. »Do we expect too much of God?« *Wisconsin State Journal*, January 12, 1974.

THE AUTHORS

AMIR MUZUR (Rijeka, 1969), graduated from the Faculty of Medicine of the University of Rijeka (1993), and obtained his master's degree in medieval studies at the Central European University (CEU) in Budapest (1996) and his doctorate in cognitive neurosciences at the International School for Advanced Studies (ISAS/SISSA) in Trieste (2000). For one year, he worked at the Laboratory for Neurophysiology of the Harvard University Medical School Department of Psychiatry in Boston. Today, he is a full professor (since 2013) and Head of the Department of Social Sciences and Humanities in Medicine (since 2008) of the University of Rijeka Faculty of Medicine, where he teaches the 'Introduction to Scientific Work', 'Introduction to Medicine and the History of Medicine', 'Altered States of Consciousness', and other courses. Since 2014, he has also been Vice Dean for Business Relations and Quality of the Faculty of Health Studies of the University of Rijeka. Since 2016, he has also held the UNESCO Chair on Social Sciences and Medical Humanities of the University of Rijeka. Muzur has published more than twenty books (on the history of Opatija and Liburnia, the history of medicine and bioethics, the popularisation of neurosciences, essays, travelogues, poetry), approximately 250 articles in scientific journals and 350 in other periodicals. At scientific and professional conferences, he has presented approximately 150 papers. He started the *Jahr* journal (editor-in-chief 2010-2014) and is a member of the editorial boards of the following journals: *The Holistic Approach to Environment*, *Jahr - Revista Europea de Bioética* (Buenos Aires; 2016-), *Journal International de Bioéthique et d'Éthique des Sciences / The International Journal of Bioethics and the Ethics of Science* (Paris; 2016-), *Ethik in der Praxis / Practical Ethics: Studien / Studies*; *Kontroversen / Controversies*; *Materialien / Documentation* (Münster; 2017-), *Journal of Applied Health Sciences / Časopis za primijenjene zdravstvene znanosti* (deputy editor-in-chief; 2017-), *Rijeka*, *Sušačka revija* and *Vinodolski zbornik*. He received first prize at the *Drago Gervais* 1999 Literary Contest. From 2005 to 2009, Muzur was mayor of Opatija. He was awarded the title of 'Mayor of the Year' (HRT Croatian Radiotelevision and HGK Croatian Chamber of Commerce, 2006), and Commendator of the Order of the Star of Italian Solidarity (from the President of the Italian Republic, 2008), and in 2011 was appointed Honorary Consul of the Republic of Poland. He is a member of the Committee for Medical Lexicography of the Croatian Academy of Sciences and Arts, the Scientific Council of the Referral Centre for Health Tourism and Medically Programmed Recreation of the Ministry of Health, the Commission for Scientific Publishing of the Ministry of Science and Education, and of the National Council for the Scientific Area of Biomedicine and Healthcare. He is Vice President of the Historical Society of Rijeka. Muzur was President of the Croatian

Bioethics Society (2012-2016). He is an honorary member of the Bioethics Society of Serbia, Director of the *Fritz Jahr* Documentation and Research Centre for European Bioethics of the University of Rijeka (since 2013), and President of the Scientific Board of the Centre of Scientific Excellence for Integrative Bioethics (since 2015). He led the following projects: 'Medical Elements in the Sacral Tradition in the Area of the Diocese of Rijeka' (Ministry of Science, Education and Sports, 2011-2014), 'Fritz Jahr and the European Roots of Bioethics: Establishing an International Scholars' Network – EuroBio*N*ethics' (Croatian Science Foundation, 2011), 'European Bioethics in Action – EuroBioAct' (Croatian Science Foundation, 2014-2017), and 'Roots of Bioethics: American and European Contributions to the Construction of a Common History' project (University of Rijeka, 2014-2018). He now leads the 'New Trends in Bioethics in Middle and South-East Europe' project (University of Rijeka; since 2019).

IVA RINČIĆ (Rijeka, 1975) graduated in 2000 in Sociology and Croatian Culture from the Department of Croatian Studies at the University of Zagreb, and defended her master's thesis in 2005 at the Faculty of Political Sciences ('The Problem of Bioethical Responsibility in Genetics: Practice in Croatia and Europe'). She defended her PhD thesis 'Theoretical Strongholds, Achievements and Perspectives of Bioethical Institutionalisation in the European Union' in 2010 at the Faculty of Philosophy in Zagreb. Since June 2001, she has been working at the Department of Social Sciences and Medical Humanities of the Rijeka University Faculty of Medicine (since 2017 as Associate Professor), and since 2014, also at the Department of Public Health of the University of Rijeka Faculty of Health Studies. She has participated at more than fifty Croatian and international conferences, published approximately fifty scientific and professional articles, and also five books on bioethics. She is a member of the editorial boards of several journals (*Filozofska istraživanja*, *Synthesis Philosophica*, *Jahr – European Journal of Bioethics*) and an associate on several Croatian and international projects. Since 2013, she has been Director of the University of Rijeka Foundation, and since 2017 also a member of the National Council for the Scientific Area of Humanities. Since 2019, she leads the 'Urban Bioethics' project (University of Rijeka).

Ethik in der Praxis/Practical Ethics

Studien/Studies

hrsg. von Prof. Dr. Hans-Martin Sass (Universität Bochum/Georgetown University Washington)
Schriftleitung: Dr. Arnd T. May

Tatjana Grützmann

Interkulturelle Kompetenz in der klinisch-ethischen Praxis

Kultursensible Ansätze zum Umgang mit interkulturellen Situationen in der Klinischen Ethikberatung

Aufgrund von Migrationsprozessen, individuellen Lebenskonzepten und multikulturellen Behandlungsteams erleben Mitarbeiter im Gesundheitswesen eine zunehmende kulturelle Diversität und damit verbunden interkulturelle Konfliktsituationen. Anhand von Fallbeispielen werden Lösungswege aufgezeigt und praxisorientierte Techniken zum professionellen Umgang mit derartigen Situationen im klinisch-ethischen Kontext vermittelt. Ansätze für eine kultursensible Ethikberatung, strukturelle Maßnahmen sowie Interkulturelle Kompetenz für Klinikmitarbeiter werden thematisiert und Experten im Rahmen von Interviews hierzu befragt.

Bd. 41, 2016, 244 S., 34,90 €, br., ISBN 978-3-643-13489-9

Hans-Martin Sass

Cultures in Bioethics

Biotopes and Bioethics are highly complex and adaptable systems of Bios. Individual bios is terminal, but the stream of Bios goes on. Basic properties of Bios such as communication and cooperation, competence and competition, contemplation and calculation, compassion and cultivation come in different shades of light and dark in individuals and species, in history and ecology. Hans-Martin Sass discusses the territories of Bios and Bioethics, based on his involvement in decades of consulting in academia, business and politics. Special attention is given to the vision and role of Bioethics in research and training, in religious and cultural traditions, and in the survival, happiness, and health of corporate, social and political bodies.

vol. 40, 2016, 260 pp., 39,90 €, pb., ISBN 978-3-643-90755-4

LIT Verlag Berlin – Münster – Wien – Zürich – London

Auslieferung Deutschland / Österreich / Schweiz: siehe Impressumsseite

Simone Horstmann
Ethik der Normalität
Zur Evolution moralischer Semantik in der Moderne
Kann es das *Normale* in der Ethik geben, muss *Normalität* auch dort Berücksichtigung finden, wo mithin einzig Normen regulativen Charakter beanspruchen? Die Arbeit fragt danach, inwieweit Normalität als moralfähige Semantik der Moderne zu verstehen ist. Dabei wird deutlich: Normalität ist der Ethik nicht fremd, sie findet sich vielfach in ethischen Anwendungsdiskursen und kann insbesondere für die Theologische Ethik als moderne Verfeinerung der Natur(rechts)-Semantik aufgefasst werden, die von natural-gegebenen Zweckstrukturen absieht und Moral als Konstruktionsleistung entwirft.
Bd. 39, 2016, 268 S., 34,90 €, br., ISBN 978-3-643-13146-1

Amir Muzur; Hans-Martin Sass (Eds.)
Fritz Jahr and the Foundations of Global Bioethics
The Future of Integrative Bioethics
Fritz Jahr, a Protestant Pastor in Halle an der Saale, coined the original term Bioethics already in 1927 and formulated in critical response to Immanuel Kant's Categorical Imperative a Bioethics Imperative for the future of integrative bioethics: "Respect every living Being as an end in itself and treat it, if possible, as such!" Leading bioethicists from America, Asia and Europe discuss Jahr's visionary concept of an ethics of "bios", integrating the ethics of land, community, health, and culture in light of global challenges in the 21. century. The book includes all 16 long forgotten articles on bioethics and ethics by Jahr from 1927 to 1947 in English translation.
vol. 37, 2012, 400 pp., 49,90 €, hc., ISBN 978-3-643-90112-5

Ralf Jox; Katja Kühlmeyer; Georg Marckmann; Eric Racine (Eds.)
Vegetative State – A Paradigmatic Problem of Modern Society
Ethical, legal, social and medical perspectives on chronic disorders of consciousness
Decision making for patients in the vegetative state is a complex issue and needs an interdisciplinary discourse that combines different perspectives. This book is based on an international neuroethics workshop for young academics and health care practitioners that took place in Munich and was funded by the German Ministry of Education and Research (BMBF). Various competitively selected participants from different countries describe their scientific contributions or their clinical experiences. Moreover experts from the field of medical ethics, neuroethics and neuroscience contribute their perspectives.
vol. 36, 2012, 216 pp., 34,90 €, pb., ISBN 978-3-643-90097-5

LIT Verlag Berlin – Münster – Wien – Zürich – London
Auslieferung Deutschland / Österreich / Schweiz: siehe Impressumsseite

Ethik in der Praxis/Practical Ethics

Kontroversen/Controversies

hrsg. von Prof. Dr. Hans-Martin Sass (Universität Bochum/Georgetown University Washington)

Schriftleitung: Dr. Arnd T. May

Timo Sauer; Valentin Schnurrer; Gisela Bockenheimer-Lucius (Hg.)
Angewandte Ethik im Gesundheitswesen
Aktuelle Entwicklungen in Theorie und Praxis
Bd. 34, 2018, 228 S., 34,90 €, br., ISBN 978-3-643-14037-1

Amir Muzur; Hans-Martin Sass (Eds.)
1926-2016 Fritz Jahr's Bioethics
A global Discourse
vol. 33, 2017, 240 pp., 29,90 €, pb., ISBN 978-3-643-90829-2

Rudolf Kautzky
Euthanasie und Gottesfrage
Medizinische Texte und theologische Provokationen. Herausgegeben und eingeleitet von Siegfried Scharrer
Bd. 32, 2.Aufl. 2014, 304 S., 29,90 €, br., ISBN 978-3-643-12679-5

Tuğsal Moğul; Alfred Simon (Hg.)
Intensiv erleben – Menschen in klinischen Grenzsituationen
Bd. 31, 2013, 144 S., 19,90 €, br., ISBN 978-3-643-11746-5

Oliver Rauprich; Jochen Vollmann (Hg.)
Die Kosten des Kinderwunsches
Interdisziplinäre Perspektiven zur Finanzierung reproduktionsmedizinischer Behandlungen
Bd. 30, 2012, 224 S., 24,90 €, br., ISBN 978-3-643-10785-5

Sylke Edith Geißendörfer
Die Selbstbestimmung des Entscheidungsunfähigen an den Grenzen des Rechts
Zur Debatte über „passive Sterbehilfe" durch Behandlungsverzicht, vormundschaftliches Genehmigungsverfahren, Patientenverfügungen und deren gesetzliche Regelungsmöglichkeiten
Bd. 29, 2009, 536 S., 39,90 €, br., ISBN 978-3-643-10049-8

Arnd T. May; Tatjana Grützmann; Jörg Brokmann (Hg.)
Patientenverfügungen in der präklinischen Notfallmedizin
Bd. 28, 2013, 192 S., 34,90 €, br., ISBN 978-3-643-10017-7

Franz Josef Illhardt (Hg.)
Die ausgeblendete Seite der Autonomie
Kritik eines bioethischen Prinzips
Bd. 27, 2008, 240 S., 34,90 €, br., ISBN 978-3-8258-1113-6

Katja Wagner-Westerhausen
Die Statusfrage in der Bioethik
Bd. 26, 2008, 248 S., 34,90 €, br., ISBN 978-3-8258-0990-4

Torbjörn Tännsjö
Zur Ethik des Tötens
Neue Anstöße zur Reflexion eines umstrittenen Problems
Bd. 25, 2006, 168 S., 16,90 €, br., ISBN 3-8258-9704-4

LIT Verlag Berlin – Münster – Wien – Zürich – London
Auslieferung Deutschland / Österreich / Schweiz: siehe Impressumsseite

Ethik in der Praxis/Practical Ethics
Materialien/Documentation
hrsg. von Prof. Dr. Hans-Martin Sass (Universität Bochum/Georgetown University Washington)
Schriftleitung: Dr. Arnd T. May

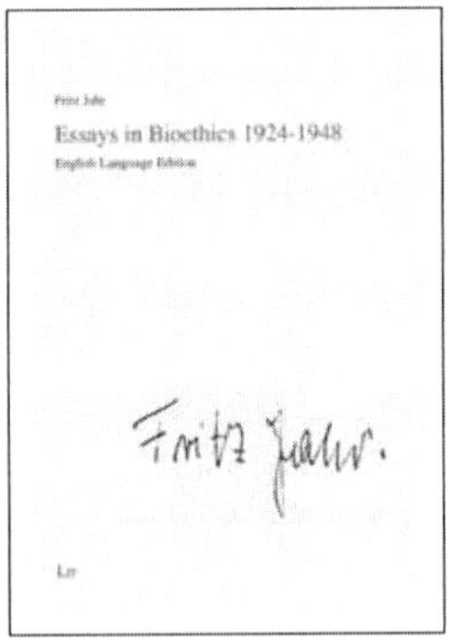

Hou Cai
The Guodian Bamboo Slips Lao Zi
English and Chinese Edition. Edited by Irene M Miller and Hans-Martin Sass
The 85 Lao Zi bamboo slips from around 300 B. C. E. are the earliest texts of what later became known as the 'Tao Te King'. They contain also the until now unknown Taoist narrative of Creation 'Great One gave Birth to Water'. These texts are very original and not yet intermingled with Confucian philosophy, governance, or ethics.
These, in 1993 discovered Bamboo Slips were translated by Professor Hou Cai initially into German. This English translation presents the Tao Bamboo Slips in modern simplified Chinese characters, with commentaries and a comparison of the modern Chinese version to the old characters. This bilingual Chinese-English publication is a contribution to the crosscultural visions and values of the New Silk Road of the 21st century.
vol. 16, 2017, 142 pp., 39,90 €, br., ISBN 978-3-643-90898-8

Fritz Jahr
Essays in Bioethics 1924 – 1948
Edited and translated by Irene M. Miller and Hans-Martin Sass
FRITZ JAHR (1895-1953), a Protestant theologian in Halle an der Saale, Germany, coined the term BIOETHICS in 1926 and defined the BIOETHICAL IMPERATIVE:
"Respect every living being on principle as an end in itself and treat it, if possible, as such". In critical dialogue with Kant's Categorical Imperative he develops the concept of modern situational bioethics. These 22 articles, written between 1924 and 1948, cover issues of ethics towards animals, plants and environments, also the ethics of social interactions with all forms of life.
The essays are of current and historical interest and serve as a guide to future global and integrated bioethics.
vol. 15, 2013, 136 pp., 29,90 €, hc., ISBN 978-3-643-90337-2

Fritz Jahr
Aufsätze zur Bioethik 1924 – 1948
Werkausgabe. Herausgegeben von Arnd T. May und Hans-Martin Sass
Bd. 14, 2. Aufl. 2013, 160 S., 24,90 €, gb., ISBN 978-3-643-12137-0

LIT Verlag Berlin – Münster – Wien – Zürich – London
Auslieferung Deutschland / Österreich / Schweiz: siehe Impressumsseite